More Virtual Field Trips

More Virtual Field Trips

Gail Cooper
and
Garry Cooper

1999
LIBRARIES UNLIMITED, INC.
and Its Division
Teacher Ideas Press
Englewood, Colorado

LIBRARIES UNLIMITED, INC.
and Its Division
Teacher Ideas Press
P.O. Box 6633
Englewood, CO 80155-6633
1-800-237-6124
www.lu.com

Library of Congress Cataloging-in-Publication Data

Cooper, Gail, 1950-
   More virtual field trips / by Gail Cooper and Garry Cooper.
   xv, 146 p. 19x26 cm.
   Includes index.
   ISBN 1-56308-770-7 (soft)
   1. Internet (Computer network) in education--United States.
2. World Wide Web (Information retrieval system)   3. School field trips--United States.   I. Cooper, Garry.   II. Title.   III. Title: Virtual field trips.
LB1044.87.C67   1999
025.06'37--dc21
                                                    99-19355
                                                         CIP

Dedication

This book is dedicated to our families, friends, teachers, and colleagues; to Alexandra Naomi Cooper, who often unintentionally reminds us how exciting it is to learn; to the teachers and staff and Principal Laurel Muhammad of Holmes School in Oak Park, who navigate with extraordinary integrity and skill among dozens of different concerns and pressures to do an outstanding job of educating students; to Jim Markunas, who successfully and bravely fought and struggled through unnecessary and unbelievable hurdles, adversities, and adversarial situations to enter high school; to Jeff Markunas for his patience and understanding; and to Charles Smith for all his help and support.

Contents

Introduction xv

Chapter 1—Virtual Time Machine 1
   1492 1
   Ancient Civilizations. 2
   Canadian History. 3
   Columbian Exposition—1893 3
   French History 4
   Greek History 5
   Holocaust. 5
   Japanese History 5
   Maritime History. 6
   Middle Ages 7
   Military History 8
   Native Americans. 11
   Renaissance. 12
   U.S. History. 12
   Women's History 19

Chapter 2—Architectural Tours 21
   Alternative Architecture 21
   American Architecture 22
   Archimedia Project 23
   Architecture Through the Ages. 23
   AutoCAD Modeling 23
   Bauhaus School of Architecture 24
   Castles and Cathedrals 24
   Chateau de Versailles. 25
   Chicago Cultural Center 26
   Columbian Exposition 26
   European Architecture 26
   Funerary Architecture 26
   Gargoyles. 26
   Gaudi, Antoni. 27
   Italian Villas 27
   New Orleans Historic Buildings 27
   Prairie School of Architecture 28
   Princeton University 28
   Roman Villa 28
   Skyscrapers. 28

Chapter 3—See the World 29
    Amazonia 29
    Arctic Circle 30
    Australia 30
    Basque Region 30
    Brazil 30
    Canada 31
    China, Republic of 31
    Ecuadorian Rain Forest 31
    Egypt 31
    France 32
    Galapagos Islands 32
    Georgia (Eastern Europe) 32
    Greenland 32
    Israel 33
    Italy 33
    Japan 33
    Madagascar 33
    Namibia 34
    Peru 34
    Spain 34
    Travel Buddies 34
    Ukraine 34
    United States 35
    United States—Alaska 36
    United States—California 36
    United States—Colorado 37
    United States—Florida 37
    United States—Georgia 38
    United States—Hawaii 38
    United States—Illinois 38
    United States—Indiana 39
    United States—Louisiana 39
    United States—Maryland 40
    United States—Minnesota 40
    United States—New Hampshire 40
    United States—New Jersey 40
    United States—New Mexico 41
    United States—New York 41
    United States—North Carolina 42
    United States—Texas 42
    United States—Virginia 43
    United States—Washington 43
    United States—Washington, D.C. 43
    United States—Wisconsin 44
    United States—Wyoming 44
    Worldwide Travel 45

Chapter 4—Down on the Farm 47
    4-H Kids Informational Dirt Road 47
    Agricultural Scavenger Hunt 47
    Alpacas 48
    Barnyard Buddies 48
    Corn World 48
    County Fair 48
    Family Farm Project 49
    Farmer's Almanac 49
    Fowl 49
    Goats 50
    Illinois Department of Agriculture 50
    The Incredible Edible Egg 50
    Livestock 50
    Miniature Donkeys 51
    National Pork Producer's Council 51
    Ohio Hokshichankiya Farm Community 51
    Sheep 52
    Texas A&M's Agropolis 52
    Virtual Ranch Tour 53
    Wheat Mania 53

Chapter 5—Mother Nature 55
    Ancient Bristlecone Pine 55
    The Animal Kingdom 56
    Arboretums and Botanic Gardens 58
    Big Bend National Park 61
    Bird-Watching 61
    Bureau of Land Management 62
    Butterfly Watching 62
    Earthquakes 63
    Glacier National Park 63
    Jurassic Reef Park 63
    Ocean 64
    Phenology 64
    Pineo Ridge Moraine—Eastern Maine 65
    Smokey the Bear 65
    Virtual Cave 65

Chapter 6—Visual Arts 67
    Animation 67
    Art Appreciation 67
    Art Lessons 68
    Art Museums 69
    Fashion and Design 71
    Gemology 72
    Mobiles and Kinetic Sculptures 73
    Photography 73

Chapter 7—Language and Performing Arts 75
Language Arts and Literature. 75
Motion Picture Industry 78
Music and Radio 78
Theaters and Plays 80

Chapter 8—Business and Industry 83
Advertising 83
International Trade 84
Manufacturing—Automobiles 85
Mining and Natural Resource Management 85
Money, Banking, and Economics 86
Newspapers and Magazines 88
Technology 89

Chapter 9—Mathematics and Logic 91
Abacus 91
Calculating Machines. 92
Captain Zoom's Math Adventure. 92
Games. 92
Math Online 92
Math Trading Cards 93
Mathematicians. 93
Plane Math 93
The Puzzling Playground 93
Quandaries and Queries 94

Chapter 10—Science 95
Anatomy 95
Archaeology 96
Aviation and Aerospace 96
Biology, Chemistry, and Genetics 97
Botany. 100
Earth and Environmental Education 100
Forensics 103
General Science 103
Inventions 107
Paleontology. 108
Physics. 109
Technology 110

Chapter 11—Health, Safety, and Fitness 111
Band Aids and Blackboards. 111
Basketball Hall of Fame. 112
Benny Goodsport 112
California State Automobile Association 112
Department of Justice 113
Dr. Rabbit's No Cavities Clubhouse 113

FDA Kid's Page. 113
Indian Health Service 114
National Crime Prevention Council. 114
National Highway Traffic Safety Administration. 114
National Institute on Drug Abuse 115
Nutrition Café 115

Chapter 12—People You Should Know 117
Alcott, Louisa May 117
Altgeld, John Peter 117
Anthony, Susan B.. 117
Antoinette, Marie 118
Armstrong, Louis 118
Armstrong, Neil 118
Ask an Expert 118
Babbage, Charles 118
Bacon, Henry 118
Ballard, Robert 119
Barton, Clara 119
Bechet, Sidney. 119
Bell, Alexander Graham. 119
Berg, Morris (Moe) 119
Bering, Vitus 119
Berry, Martha 119
Bini, Dante 119
Blume, Judy 119
Bly, Nellie. 120
Boone, Daniel 120
Bowie, James 120
Brett, Jan 120
Bryant, Gridley J. F.. 120
Bulfinch, Charles 120
Burnham, Daniel 120
Cabrillo, Juan 120
Calamity Jane 121
Capote, Truman 121
Carnegie, Andrew 121
Carson, Christopher Houston (Kit) 121
Cassidy, Butch. 121
Catt, Carrie Chapman 121
Cauchy, Augustin Louis. 121
Cerf, Vinton 121
Cermak, Anton 121
Clark, William. 122

Chapter 12—People You Should Know (*continued*)

Cleburne, Patrick 122
Clinton, Hillary Rodham 122
Cochran, Jacqueline 122
Cody, William Frederick (Buffalo Bill) 122
Columbus, Christopher 123
Cook, Captain James 123
Cornet, Antoni Gaudi 123
Cousteau, Jacques 123
Cray, Seymour 123
Crockett, Davy 123
De Gaulle, Charles 123
De Paola, Tomie 123
DeSoto, Hernando 124
Domino, Antoine (Fats) 124
Donovan, William 124
Douglass, Frederick 124
Drake, Francis 124
Earhart, Amelia 124
Earp, Wyatt 124
Edison, Thomas Alva 125
Einstein, Albert 125
Elmslie, George Grant 125
Fermi, Enrico 125
Ferraro, Geraldine 125
Field, Marshall 126
Fisher, Carl 126
Fisher, Irving 126
Fitzgerald, F. Scott 126
Ford, Robert 126
Forrest, Nathan Bedford 126
Forrester, Jay 126
Frank, Anne 126
Franklin, Benjamin 127
French, Daniel Chester 127
Freud, Sigmund 127
Galileo 127
Gates, Bill 128
Gaudi, Antoni 128
Gauss, Carl Friedrich 128
Giraffe Project 128
Goddard, Robert 129
Goldberg, Reuben Lucius (Rube) 129
Grant, Ulysses S. 129
Greenhow, Rose O'Neal 129
Gropius, Walter 129
Guerin, Jules 129
Guthrie, Janet 130

Gwinnett, Button 130
Heaney, Seamus 130
Hearst, William Randolph 130
Hendrix, Jimi 130
Hewlett, William 130
Hill, Virginia 130
Holabird and Root 130
Holliday, Doc 130
James, Jesse 130
Janus, Allen 131
Jefferson, Thomas 131
Jobs, Steve 131
Jones, Quincy 131
Kahlo, Frida 131
King, Jr., Martin Luther 131
Klee, Paul 131
La Salle, Rene 131
Lafayette, James Armistead 131
Lafitte, Jean 131
Latrobe, Benjamin Henry 131
Lawrence, T. E. 132
Levine, Philip 132
Lewis, C. S. 132
Lewis, Meriwether 132
Lincoln, Abraham 132
Lincoln, Mary Todd 133
The Lone Ranger 133
Louis XIV 133
McArthur, Douglas 133
McKane, John 133
McKinley, William 133
Marconi, Guglielmo 133
Marsalis Family 134
Masterson, William 134
Metcalfe, Robert 134
Meyer, Anne 134
Michelangelo 134
Miller, John 134
Milosz, Czeslaw 134
Mitchell, Billy 134
Mitchell, Maria 135
Moran, Thomas 135
Morton, Ferdinand (Jelly Roll) 135
Mubarak, Hosney 135
Muybridge, Eadweard James 135
Napoleon 135

Chapter 12—People You Should Know (*continued*)

Nassy, Josef 135
Newton, Isaac 135
Owens, Jesse 135
Packard, David 136
Palladio, Andrea 136
Palmer, Potter 136
Pascal, Blaise 136
Paulsen, Gary 136
Percy, Walker 136
Pinkerton, Allan 136
Pinsky, Robert 136
Pocahontas 136
Pullman, George 136
Purcell, William Gray 137
Rickenbacker, Eddie 137
Rogers, Will 137
Rolfe, John 137
Roosevelt, Theodore 137
Saint Gaudens, Augustus 137
Schultz, Charles 138
Seuss, Dr. 138
Sherman, William T. 138
Slocum, Joshua 138
Smith, Adam 138
Smith, Captain John 139
Stowe, Harriet Beecher 139
Sullivan, Louis 139
Thompson, William Hale 139
Tubman, Harriet 139
Twentieth Century Academy of Achievement 139
Van der Rohe, Lugwig Mies 140
Van Gogh, Vincent 140
Walker, C. J. 140
Washington, Harold 140
Welles, Orson 140
Wharton, Edith 140
Wilder, Laura Ingalls 140
Williams, Tennessee 140
Wright, Frank Lloyd 140
Yeager, Charles 140

Index 141

Introduction

Both the Internet and the field of education are undergoing rapid, dynamic changes. Classroom teachers and parents are being urged by administrators, government, and society and by the children themselves to utilize the Internet. However, although its potential is enormous for enhancing learning, it can still be misused or underutilized. Our goal is to continue to maximize the Internet's potential by making resources readily available and encouraging children to be excited about and committed to their education.

As the Internet has continued its amazing growth, thousands of new opportunities for virtual field trips have appeared. *More Virtual Field Trips* covers additional sites and opportunities that have appeared in the year since our original book, *Virtual Field Trips*, was published. Together, the two books provide hours of educational opportunities for you and your students to travel throughout the world and back and forth in time, study natural phenomena, and participate in cultural and scientific activities with professionals and worldwide classrooms.

As in the original *Virtual Field Trips*, we have steered readers away from those Internet sites that are either thinly disguised advertisements, are inappropriate for K–12 students, or are run by people or organizations that seem, to put it charitably, suspect. We've used our contacts—readers of *Virtual Field Trips*, educators, parents, and other sources—to find the field trips that are the most useful and stimulating and meet the specific goals and interests of educators. *More Virtual Field Trips* will continue to save our readers hours of frustration. For example, we've included a chapter titled "People You Should Know"—and have shielded you from running into people you *don't* want to know.

We've also added new trips and topics that reflect current curricular requirements and goals, such as business, women's history, conflict resolution, and multiculturalism. We've added trips for physically and emotionally challenged students and those who wish to get to know them better. You'll also find, per your requests, more physical education, health and safety, rural, and architectural field trips.

An icon of a school house and school bell is used to identify URLs of sites that are exclusively for students in primary grades.

As always, just like ancient Egypt, the Wild West, Japan, Hawaii, Salem, Rube Goldberg, Vincent Van Gogh, the U.S. Department of Justice, and the bottom of the ocean, we're just a few taps of the keyboard and a mouse-click away, and we're happy to answer any questions or "talk" with you. Our e-mail addresses are gailc1@ix.netcom.com and gcoop@ix.netcom.com.

CHAPTER 1

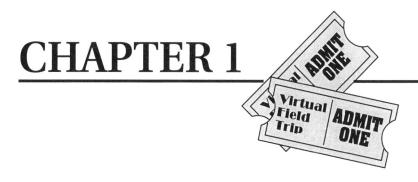

VIRTUAL TIME MACHINE

Take your students back through time and experience the cultures, wonders, clothes, architecture, and manners—or lack thereof—of the past. Together, you can experience ancient cultures, two world wars, the Wild West, the Civil War, and the French Revolution and still have time to sit on the beach waiting for Columbus to arrive. While he's been trying to "discover" America, you and your class have already been up to Canada to visit with the First Nations, have gone back to the Renaissance and Middle Ages, and have learned about the centuries of American history that occurred before Columbus even left Spain.

1492

http://sunsite.unc.edu/expo/1492.exhibit/Intro.html

If you are looking to put Christopher Columbus' "discovery" of America in perspective, pay a visit to this exhibit from the University of North Carolina. Students will learn about the several advanced civilizations that were already here, as well as the politics, culture, and perspective of the entire Mediterranean world from which Columbus sailed. This even-handed account of Columbus's arrival in America has a collection of texts, graphics, and photos, adaptable to all grade level curricula. For example, the explanation and pictures of the two coats of arms—one that Queen Isabella gave to Columbus and the other that he altered to suit his own ego—provide both an explanation of how to read coats of arms and an intimate portrait of the individual perspectives of the Queen and Columbus. Columbus changed the colors and added a continent to the Queen's island.

ANCIENT CIVILIZATIONS

Architecture

See Chapter 2—Archimedia Project, Architecture Through the Ages, AutoCAD Modeling, *and* Roman Villa; *and* Chapter 3—Israel.

Culture

http://www.cc.emory.edu/CARLOS/ODYSSEY/index.html

This teacher-friendly tour of the ancient Near East, Egyptian, Greek, and Roman cultures is designed to meet curriculum content and process guidelines from Georgia and New York, so it is packed with inquiry-based questions. For example, after the site discusses the hunter-gatherers of the ancient Near East, students are asked to name any other hunter-gatherers they can think of. The tour, a collaboration of Emory University's Michael C. Carlos Museum and the Memorial Art Gallery of the University of Rochester, resembles a multimedia textbook. The combination of questions, games, maps, music, sounds, original documents, and high-resolution photographs of archaeological objects make the past interesting and relevant.

Florence and Tuscany

See Chapter 12—Galileo.

Greece and Rome—Perseus Project

http://www.perseus.tufts.edu

Tufts University's Perseus Project is sponsored by the university's Classics Department and supported by many foundations, government agencies, and corporations, including the National Science Foundation, the National Endowment for the Arts, the National Endowment for the Humanities, and the Getty Foundation. The project is essentially a state-of-the-art, multimedia humanities library concentrating on ancient Greek culture. Materials include ancient texts, philological tools, maps, illustrated art catalogs, and secondary essays. More than 70 museums have shared pictures of their art objects, including coins, architecture, and vases. Primary texts include Homer's *Odyssey,* available in either English or classical Greek. The project now includes ancient Rome, and there are plans to expand into other areas of the humanities. Be sure to take a walk around ancient Athens while you are visiting.

Greek and Roman Stagecraft

See Chapter 7—Theaters and Plays—Ancient Greek and Roman Stagecraft.

Mesopotamia

http://saturn.sron.ruu.nl/~jheise/akkadian

Travel to ancient Mesopotamia, the area now encompassed by Iraq and a portion of Syria. John Heise, an astrophysicist in the Netherlands, shares his publications about this ancient area, much of which concentrate on the Akkadian language and cuneiform writing. The information, largely geared toward upper-level students, will allow them to gain a comprehensive knowledge of this ancient land and culture. Younger students will enjoy seeing actual examples of ancient writing.

Mississippi Moundbuilders

http://www.cr.nps.gov/delta

The National Park Service sponsors this tour of the lower Mississippi delta and the ancient Moundbuilders—the first intensive farmers of North America's eastern woodlands. The tour includes views of the remaining mounds and provides interesting information about the culture of these ancient peoples as well as the role of the Mississippi River in the development of their society.

CANADIAN HISTORY

See Maritime History—Maritime Museum of British Columbia *and* Native Americans.

COLUMBIAN EXPOSITION—1893

http://users.vnet.net/schulman/Columbian/columbian.html

Take your students to the Columbian Exposition in Chicago. It may take some time to get there because passenger planes have not yet been invented. It will take you 32 hours from Boston and 211 days from Berlin. More than 27.5 million people will attend at an admission price of 50 cents for adults and 25 cents for children ages 6–12. If you want to take pictures with your own camera, it will cost another $2.00 per day, and just about anything you want to do will cost extra, so bring plenty of spending money. For example, admission to the Algerian Theater is 25 cents, and the balloon ride is $2.00. The exposition covers 633 acres in Chicago's Jackson Park, and if you don't want to walk, you will have to pay 50 cents for a ride on the Venetian gondolas, 25 cents for the steamship, or 10 cents to ride the rail. Be sure to stop at the Midway—the first area deliberately made into a self-contained entertainment district. You will see things invented specifically for the exposition, such as the first elevated electric railway and Ferris wheel, and things to eat that have never been on the market before, such as Cracker Jacks, shredded wheat, and diet soda. Administrators of this site also describe the art and architecture designed especially for the event.

FRENCH HISTORY

Chateau de Versailles

http://www.chateauversailles.fr

English- or French-speaking guides will take your students on a tour of the buildings and grounds of the Chateau de Versailles, courtesy of the Museum of French History. The 2,060 acres of grounds, organized around the 100-acre Grand Canal, include 12 miles of roads; 200,000 trees; 50 fountains; and gardens and groves designed by André Lenôtre, an expert in botany, architecture, and painting who perfected the model of French-style gardens. Students interested in engineering will be fascinated by the water system, a 120-mile network of channels, trenches, and aqueducts devised by Louis XIV's mathematicians and engineers. Be sure to visit the Chapel Royal, a unique combination of Gothic and Baroque architecture designed by Jules Hardoin-Mansart. If your students prefer to spend the day with Louis XIV, they will have to adhere to a very strict schedule—the King's day must be perfectly timed so that his officers know exactly what to do and when to do it. Louis XIV arises at 8:30 A.M.,when the First Valet de Chambre declares, "It is time, Sire!" During the *levee*, or ceremonial rising, doctors, family, and a few favored friends make sure the King is washed, combed, shaved, dressed, and fed. Preparation for mass begins at 10:00 A.M., when a procession forms in the Hall of Mirrors. During the 30-minute mass, the choir known as Chapel Music sings new compositions from Jean-Baptiste Lully, Michel-Richard de Lalande, and other composers of the day. At 11:00 A.M. the King returns to his apartments and holds council in his cabinet. He dines alone from 1:00 P.M. to 2:00 P.M., so your students will have to find some other way to entertain themselves—perhaps by wandering around and meeting such people as Marie Antoinette, Napoleon, or Charles de Gaulle. Be sure to make it back in time for the King's afternoon program beginning promptly at 2:00 P.M. You never know what he has planned—it could entail anything from a walk through the gardens to hunting. Take some time to grab a snack because dinner will not be served until 10:00 P.M. The day ends at 11:30 with the conchee, a public ritual that is basically the reverse and shortened version of the levee. And don't forget to take a look at some of the works of art while you are wandering around. Due to the Chateau's dual role as a royal residence and a museum, there are many paintings, drawings, sculptures, furniture, instruments, and other objets d'art from the Middle Ages through the twentieth century.

France's Age of Enlightenment

See Chapter 6—Art Museums—France's Age of Enlightenment.

GREEK HISTORY

See Chapter 6—Fashion and Design—Greek Costume Through the Ages *and* Gemology—Greek Jewelry—5,000 Years of Tradition.

HOLOCAUST

See also Chapter 12—Frank, Anne.

Simon Wiesenthal Center

http://www.wiesenthal.com

The Simon Wiesenthal Center in Los Angeles, California, is dedicated to keeping the memory of the Holocaust alive and to alerting people to the dangers of racism and hatred in modern society. Each day, a different child of the Holocaust is featured, with a photograph and detailed story. There is also up-to-date information on current hate groups, including an interview with a skinhead, and extensive bibliographies.

United States Holocaust Memorial Museum

http://www.ushmm.org/index.html

The U.S. Holocaust Memorial Museum in Washington, D.C., is usually so crowded that you have to buy tickets well in advance of your visit. But with this Website, your class can visit at any time. The online exhibits represent the museum's extensive collection of materials, including official documents, photographs, magazine covers, identification cards, and newspaper clippings—all of which bring home the reality of the Holocaust from the institutional to the personal level. The tours cover not only the horrors and villains but the everyday Christian and Jewish heroes as well. Current tours include the art of Josef Nassy, a black expatriate of Jewish descent who was confined in a camp for three years; Father Jacques, a Carmelite friar who hid several Jewish boys in his French school in 1937; the 1932 Olympics in Berlin; and excerpts from official war crime trials. The museum also allows online access to its photographic and document collections. Teachers will want to check the section entitled *Learn About the Holocaust,* which provides teaching guidelines, background information, discussion questions, and an annotated videography. The section on *Children of the Holocaust* presents the tightening legal, social, and geographic noose as it affected children.

JAPANESE HISTORY

See also Chapter 3—Japan.

Japanese American Museum

http://www.lausd.k12.ca.us/janm

The Japanese American Museum in San Diego is the only U.S. museum dedicated to sharing the experience of Americans of Japanese ancestry. The museum's digital exhibits concentrate largely on the era of World War II internment camps. There is a collection of correspondence sent to Clara Breed from teenagers and young adults living in the camps that covers daily life, thoughts, and family separations. Breed, a San Diego librarian who knew many of the children prior to their internment, was considered by them to be a lifeline to the outside world. One child writes: "Thank you Miss Breed, for asking questions because it has helped me a lot for than [*sic*] I know this letter has something of interest to you." The exhibits, which include movie and audio clips about the Japanese American experience, are powerful reminders of how fragile freedom can be.

 MARITIME HISTORY

Maritime Museum of British Columbia

http://www.mmbc.bc.ca

Students can spend hours wandering the various galleries of this museum learning the story of British Columbia from the mid-eighteenth century explorations of Captain James Cook to the advent of the Canadian Pacific passenger steamships. They will even be able to spend some time with the British Royal Navy. Early explorers will be willing to recreate some of their famous voyages and share plans and specifications of their ships. Our personal favorite was Captain Joshua Slocum, who shares the story of his voyage on a small barque that became stranded on a sandbar off the coast of Brazil in 1886. Using a 35-foot hand-built canoe pulled from the wreckage, he traveled 5,000 miles to bring his family safely back to New York City. Be sure to spend some time on the Golden Hind with Sir Francis Drake, search for the Northwest Passage with Captain James Cook, or dress warmly and join Vitus Bering as he discovers the Bering Strait and Sea. The less adventuresome may want to hang around the museum, which has one of the most extensive ship databases in the world.

Minnesota Historical Society

http://www.mnhs.org/index.html

Administrators of this site claim that the real treasures at the Minnesota Historical Society Museum are the old stories of Lake Superior maritime history dating back to the era of exploration and fur trading in 1680. Due to the extremely cold temperatures of the lake, many of these ship-wrecked vessels have been preserved and are available for "cyber tours." Each tour is complete with underwater photographs, detailed descriptions of the ship's construction and history, and stories of the shipwreck. Many of these tragedies have historical significance and resulted in the passage of the maritime laws still in place today.

Tour of the Belle

http://www.thc.state.tx.us/Belle/index.html

The Texas Historical Commission will take your students on a tour of the Belle, one of the earliest shipwrecks to occur in North America. They will tell you all about the excavation of the ship, which lasted for almost one year, and show you some of the finds, which include the ship's hull, cannons, and even the skeleton of a crew member. Through the use of technology, scientists have been able to reconstruct an image of what the sailor might have looked like, and armed with a DNA sample, they are currently searching for his descendants. You are welcome to watch the conservationists at work as they restore items found in the ship that sank in Matagorda Bay in 1686 during an expedition led by René La Salle. History buffs will want to check the brief biographies of La Salle and King Louis XIV and view the exhibits of naval artillery used during the seventeenth century. A newsletter for teachers (*Journeys*) archived on site contains resources, lesson plans, and interactive activities that encourage the use of inquiry-based learning in connection with the exhibit.

MIDDLE AGES

See also Chapter 2—Castles and Cathedrals—Medieval Castles.

Medieval England

http://www.regia.org/index.html

Travel back in time to Britain (950–1066 C.E.) courtesy of the Regia Anglorum, a worldwide "living history society" dedicated to authentically recreating medieval England. The tour begins at the Manor of Drengham, where the Earl of Godwin tells you about his duties of law and order and military obligations to the King. (Teachers of younger students may want to avoid the section on weaponry.) The Earl will take your students hunting in the wilds of Swinwudu, the local forest, where he'll show them the flora and fauna. Or feel free to wander through the village of Wichamstow and drop in on some of the local craftspeople. If you want to bring home some mementos of your trip, it would be wide to stop and visit the monier—it's hard to figure out what things are worth in a barter economy, so you will need his help. Our favorite craftsperson was Edgar oe Banuyrhta, who works with bones and antlers (plastic hasn't been invented yet) and loves to show off his tools. He showed us how to make a comb. (Use antler—it's much stronger than bone.) The local baker will tell you about feasts and fasts, including appropriate etiquette. If you prefer, stop in at Duddas Drenchus (Dudda's Tavern) and listen to some storytellers or partake in some dice, board games, or riddles. (It's said that a warrior's word skills are supposed to be as good as his weaponry skills.) You probably won't want to compete in the local sports because the rules are much different from what you might expect. For example, in a swimming competition, it's considered fair to try and drown your opponent, and in their version of the tug-of-war, teams tug on an animal skin over an open fire. The more faint of heart may prefer to walk down to the quay and chat with the shipwright or take a ship to the lands of the Vikings and Normans.

MILITARY HISTORY

See also U.S. History—PBS American Experience Series *and* Chapter 3— United States—California—Fort McArthur Museum *and* Nike Missile Site.

American Revolution

See U.S. History—Federal Reserve Bank—American Currency Exhibit *and* Georgia.

Civil War

See also U.S. History—Federal Reserve Bank—American Currency Exhibit *and* Georgia *and* Chapter 3— United States—Illinois—Chicago's Graveyards.

Civil War Tour 1

http://Civilwarmini.com

A review of this site states, "It's as if someone had gone through a library of Civil War books and dog-eared all the cool facts and intriguing stories." For example, a Confederate lieutenant who had surrendered to Union forces at Cumberland Gap requested years later on his deathbed that his grandson return to the Gap in 100 years, stand at the pinnacle, and curse the Yankees for five minutes. And the grandson did as he was requested on September 9, 1963, exactly 100 years later! Take your students on a tour of the entire Civil War, with intimate details provided through letters, diaries, literature, and documents. In between the social, political, economic, and military battles, students can listen to songs from the era such as "Turkey in the Straw" or relax with a *True/False* or a *Name the Celebrity Quiz.* Do you know which American author served as a nurse in the war? (Hint: She wrote *Little Women.*)

Civil War Tour 2

http://www.access.digex.net/~bdboyle/cw.html
http://users.iamdigex.net/bdboyle/cw.html

Think of Civil War aficionado Bryan Boyle's site as a worldwide information center that people interested in any aspect of the war can visit whenever they want to obtain the latest news or Civil War information. If you want recipes for beef jerky or swamp cabbage stew, family histories of soldiers, regimental histories, or Civil War music, pay a visit. A considerable part of the site is devoted to Civil War reenactments, presenting material and links to the hundreds of people and organizations who seek to keep the experience of the war alive by holding pageants, publishing papers, conducting research, networking, and holding meetings. Your class can read the latest copy of the *Civil War Reenactment Gazette* to get a feel for daily life or a military official's detailed analysis of a Civil War battle that assesses the strategy and military and psychological fitness of both sides.

Civil War Tour 3

http://californiacentralcoast.com/commun/map/civil/civil.html

One of the most interesting aspects of this tour, sponsored by the Civil War Network, is its coverage of women in the war. Students will be able to meet such influential women as Harriet Beecher Stowe, Clara Barton, Rose O'Neal Greenhow, Mary Todd Lincoln, and Mrs. James Devereaux. There are also state battle maps, battle statistics, information on Confederate flags, and primary source documents.

United States Air Force

http://www.af.mil/aflinkjr

Once you gain access to this top-secret Air Force junior site with your own code name, an official virtual pass will be issued, allowing entrance to the game or media room, lab, airfield, or post office. The graphics and sounds are so incredible that students probably won't realize that the materials are also educational. The game room has a coloring book, word search, and the Air Force version of *Mad Libs* in which students write their own news stories. Students can learn the story of the Air Force at the media lab and meet such notables as Brigadier General Billy Mitchell, who came up with the idea to use airplanes in battle; Captain Eddie Rickenbacker, whose expertise as a race car driver helped him become the best pilot in World War I; Dr. Robert Goddard, the first man to build a rocket; Captain Charles Yeager, the first to break the sound barrier; and Commander Neil Armstrong, the first person to set foot on the moon. Students can also listen to Air Force music and learn about some of the more notable planes, such as the B29 Superfortress or the C-5 Galaxy, which can carry 1,200,000 ¼-pound hamburgers. Stop by the airfield and learn about the elements of flight and use your knowledge to construct paper airplanes. Pay attention— if you pass the exam, the Air Force has a special surprise for you. With any luck, you will have time to visit the post office and send an e-mail card to a friend.

See also Chapter 9—Captain Zoom's Math Adventure.

War of 1812

See Chapter 3—United States—Louisiana—New Orleans.

World War I

http://www.worldwar1.com

Trenches on the Web, a labor of love by Mike Iavarone, vice president of information technology at First Chicago Bank, contains just about anything you might want to know about the people, places, events, and politics of World War I. The collection of primary and secondary source documents is constantly expanding. Iavarone is a self-described "historical technician" rather than a historian, and as a result, the collection is one of the most unbiased and apolitical students are likely to encounter. Check the *Reference Library* for a complete listing of available materials, use the search function if you are looking for specific materials, or take one of the theme-based tours. There are instructions for translating the materials into French, German, Italian, Portuguese, and Spanish. Diverse materials include firsthand accounts of the Second Battle of Ypres, the paintings of Mary Riter Hamilton, the music of Lieutenant James Reese Europe, and the sonnets of John Allan Wyeth, as well as German and Italian war poetry, scanned images of actual wartime newspapers, casualty statistics, American Expeditionary Force records, memorabilia, and British Trench maps.

World War II

See also Holocaust *and* Japanese History.

World War II—Drop Zone Museum

http://www.thedropzone.org

This oral and pictorial history project has been established to honor the U.S. army's elite World War II infantry units—the paratroopers, glider pilots, and rangers. There are rare photo collections of Normandy taken from the lens of a captured German camera, Ranger Medic Frank South's description of the landings and assault on the cliffs of Pointe du Hoc on D day, virtual scrapbooks, oral histories by theater, and artifacts, as well as materials on the Triple Nickles—America's first African American paratroopers. Note: Several of the first-person descriptions are graphic. We recommend you screen this site ahead of time.

World War II—Women's Air Force Service Pilots

http://www.wasp-wwii.org/wasp/home.htm

During World War II, a group of female pilots, known as the WASPs, became the first women in history to fly American military aircraft. This site pays tribute to this select group of women (25,000 women applied, 1,830 were accepted, and only 1,074 earned their "wings") ,using primary source documents, stories, and texts. Students will be inspired by Jacqueline Cochran, who rose from sweeping beauty parlors to become director of the WASPs. Cochran still holds more distance and speed records than any pilot, living or dead. Lesser known service women are also profiled in personal scrapbooks and first- and secondhand accounts of their training and Air Force life. Students can hear songs; see pictures; obtain statistics about the planes the women flew; and view original diplomas, letters, flight checklists, and other materials. There are also audio speeches by General Henry "Hap" Arnold, Jacqueline Cochran, Janet Reno, and Chuck Yeager honoring the pilots.

NATIVE AMERICANS

See also U.S. History—Georgia *and* Chapter 3—United States—New Mexico.

Cherokee Tribe

http://www.indians.org/welker/cherokee.htm

The story of the Cherokee Indians is one of the most shameful and sad in our nation's history. Uprooted from their native lands in the Carolinas, they and other tribes were forced to march on the long Trail of Tears to arid Oklahoma. Your students can read a collection of eloquent speeches from Cherokee leaders such as Chief Chickamauga who says that, "Whole Indian nations have melted before the advance of the white man like snowballs in the sun." Despite the sorrowful tale, Cherokee folktales are full of wonderful stories that explain such things as why the Opossum's tail is bare. Several folktales, as well as other Cherokee literature, are available on-site. Your students can learn about Cherokee laws, language, and history, and links are available to collections of Cherokee art.

Luxton Museum of the Plains Indians

http://www.rescol.ca/collections/luxton

This Banff, Alberta, institution, sponsored by the Buffalo Nations Cultural Society, allows students to relive the life of nineteenth century Plains Indians. Students can travel back to the days when people followed the buffalo herds, hauled equipment by travois, and scraped hides for tepees. The tour is divided into 20 modules within four sections—*history and background, hunter-warrior, spiritual life,* and *daily life*—and the precise, intimate details will appeal to students. For example, immediately after birth, Plains Indians buried the afterbirth by a young, strong tree, so that the tree and the child could grow together for the rest of the child's life. Each module is designed for a 50-minute class and includes texts, photos, short comprehension tests, and extended learning activities for each grade from third to seventh grade.

Virtual Keeping House: A First Nation's Gallery

http://www.sicc.sk.ca/keepinghouse or /elders

The Virtual Keeping House: A First Nation's Gallery was established in 1972 by the Saskatchewan Indian Cultural Centre (SICC). SICC's mission is to "strengthen and support the overall education, retention, and revitalization of the five First Nation's languages in Saskatchewan." To further this effort, the site displays paintings and artifacts that encompass the traditions of the three groups of Cree-speaking people, including the Dene of northern Saskatchewan and the Sioux of the Dakotas. Photographs and descriptions of the culture portray baskets, blankets, carvings, food, drums, footwear, games and sports, men's and women's wear, ornaments, pottery, and sculpture. The alternative path (elders) contains stories told by more than 100 tribal elders, with their photographs. Says First Nation Piapot Henry Ironchild, "The only way for our youngsters to learn is for us to tell them what our elders told us: to love one another, tell about our Indian ceremonies, the traditional dances. Long ago, you didn't get information from the Elders for nothing. Sweet grass and tobacco were given in exchange." The information on this site is also provided in French.

RENAISSANCE

http://www.twingroves.district96.K12.il.us/Renaissance/VirtualRen.html

Once you step through the portal back to the Renaissance, you will be so busy that you may not make it back in time for the bus. Some of your students may not want to stay too long, once they learn the harsh Elizabethan laws and the consequences of defying them. The tour, developed by students at Twin Groves Junior High in Buffalo Grove, Illinois, is conducted by location or character. Hang around town and visit with the craftspeople, the merchants, and the bankers. (Pritchard the Glassmaker is currently working on a fluted bowl commissioned by the Medici family.) Or, pay a visit to the Sistine Chapel, where Lorenzo de' Medici will tell you about Michelangelo's life. We were lucky enough to run into the master's assistant, who told us how the chapel was painted. The more theatrically minded may prefer to spend some time at the Globe Theater and learn about its history, or eavesdrop on the conversations between Anne (Shakespeare's wife) and Mouse (Richard Burbage's wife). Take good care of yourself, or you may wind up in the Hospital of the Innocents. Just about everyone receives the same diagnosis—an imbalance between the four basic elements of life, which is usually treated with leeches. As bad as this may be, it is preferable to the techniques employed by the barber/surgeon. Other tours include the Tower of London, a clothing shop, the local tavern, and the Mount Joy School of Boys, where you can learn some Renaissance school yard insults. Progress, however, is underway at the University of Padua, where the staff is currently working on modern inventions such as clocks, eyeglasses, and the flush toilet.

U.S. HISTORY

See also Military History—United States Air Force, Native Americans, *and* Women's History; *and* Chapter 3—United States—Central Intelligence Agency, Virginia, *and* Wyoming.

American West—Colorado Lore, Legend, and Fact

http://www.ionet.net/~jellenc

Travel back in time to nineteenth-century Colorado and experience the heyday and decline of the mining economy. You might want to first stop at Leadville's *Crystal Carnival* in the Ice Palace, but be sure to get there before the warm weather. The palace, which is over 1 acre in size, is constructed of 5,000 tons of ice blocks with 90-foot towers. Once it melts, it will never be replaced because Congress is about to repeal the Sherman Silver Purchase Act, which will cripple Colorado's economy. Keep a close watch over your students when you visit the mining camp at Creede—it's said that "some of her citizens would take sweepstake prizes at a hog show." However, who would pass up the opportunity to spend time with such residents as Bob Ford, Bat Masterson, and Calamity Jane? There's almost always a room available at the Palace Hotel—a 16-square-foot shack with hanging blankets for doors. (What do you expect for $1.00 a night?) Wander anywhere through the state, and you are sure to meet somebody interesting, such as Doc Susie, the high-country physician, or various outlaws, gamblers, and lawmen, including Butch Cassidy, Wyatt Earp and his friend Doc Holliday, Soapy Smith (one of America's first con men), or Poker Alice. Those who prefer nature can visit the high-country gallery, the penny postcard collection, the alpine tundra in the Rockies, or the Colorado fourteeners (55 mountain peaks over 14,000 feet in height).

American West—James-Younger Gang

http://www3.islandnet.com/~the-gang/index.html

The James-Younger Gang is a not-for-profit educational and historical Missouri organization that serves as a source of exchange for writers, historians, and family descendants of the infamous group that thrilled and terrorized the American West. Individually and as a gang, their robberies took place from Texas to Minnesota and West Virginia to Missouri, and every one is listed along with photographs, woodcuts, and drawings. There are photographs and stories about the James and Younger brothers as well as "that dirty rat" Bob Ford, the victims, and the women in their lives. Due to the participation of descendants, there are unusual items, photographs, and stories at this site, such as the violin one gang member learned to play while in jail.

American West Tour

http://www.AmericanWest.com

If your class has a hankerin' to visit anywhere in the historical or modern American West, here's the place to begin your tour. This massive site lets you plan your journey by choosing one of 22 states or subjects, starting from the frontier and pioneer days. Your students will participate in many notable events as they travel along various western trails with Native Americans, pioneers, trappers, scouts, and even outlaws and gunslingers. There are original maps to guide you in your travels, including the 1821 map of the Santa Fe Trail, the 1835 map of the Oregon Trail, and the Pony Express Route of 1800. Those who want to sign on with the Pony Express will have to meet the qualifications posted in the original advertisement—"Wanted. Young, skinny, wiry fellows. Not over 18. Must be expert riders. Willing to risk death daily. Orphans preferred." Feel free to wander around Tombstone, Arizona, the Black Hills of South Dakota, or Dodge City, Kansas, but be sure to follow the local laws. For example, in Dodge City, guns cannot be worn north of the "deadline" (the railroad track). You may want to spend some time with James Bowie, Davy Crockett, Daniel Boone, Kit Carson, or Buffalo Bill.

See also Chapter 12—Cody, William Frederick (Buffalo Bill).

Civil Rights Movement

See Chapter 3—United States—Maryland.

Civil War

See Chapter 1—Military History.

Coney Island

http://naid.sppsr.ucla.edu/coneyisland

Take a historic tour of New York's Coney Island, one of the early-twentieth-century's most famous amusement parks. The tour, based on free-lance photographer and writer Jeffrey Stanton's forthcoming book, includes illustrated historical articles about New York; the amusement park industry (including the birth of the roller coaster); luxury nineteenth-century hotels; and an introduction to John McKane, the corrupt politician responsible for transforming the island from a natural resource into a neon dreamland. Click anywhere on the interactive maps to tour the amusement park and surrounding areas, such as the Bowery and Surf Avenue.

Federal Reserve Bank—American Currency Exhibit

http://www.frbsf.org/econedu/games/index.html

The Federal Reserve Bank of San Francisco explains U.S. history through its currency. Students can travel back in time beginning with the struggle for independence, through the Civil War, the Industrial Revolution, the era of metal standards, and up to the current age of the global economy. Make sure they bring their backpacks because they will need many types of currency such as the Massachusetts 12 Pence (1776) engraved by Paul Revere, the Spanish milled dollar, "broken" bank notes, the $\frac{1}{3}$ dollar engraved by Ben Franklin and issued to finance the American Revolution, and Confederate currency issued between 1861 and 1865 (northerners also printed this currency and circulated it throughout the South, which led to one of the greatest inflationary periods in U.S. history). A separate tour is based on the artistry of paper currency. Students will learn how currency artists incorporate portraits, shields, borders, monuments, buildings, plants, cornucopias, seals, historical events, and allegories into their works, using tools that have remained basically unchanged since the fifteenth century. They will learn that only two women's portraits have ever appeared on currency (Martha Washington and Pocahontas) and that corn, cotton, wheat, and tobacco—the four agricultural products of colonial America—are always depicted.

See also Chapter 8—Money, Banking, and Economics.

Georgia

http://www.ngeorgia.com/history

Northern Georgia's history encompasses the Creek and Cherokee Indians as well as the American Revolution, the Civil War, and Reconstruction, and now you can take your students to both present-day and historical places. Did you know that in 1828 Georgia had its own gold rush? Learn about the area through maps, photographs, timelines, articles, and biographies of people such as Hernando de Soto, Declaration of Independence signatory Button Gwinnett; Civil War heroes Patrick Cleburne and Nathan Bedford Forrest; William Tecumseh Sherman ("who was and still is the most hated and despised man in the history of Georgia"); and Martha Berry, who was largely responsible for founding public schools in northern Georgia.

Jamestown, Virginia

http://www.apva.org

A 1907 guidebook to Jamestown, Virginia, states: "The Far East has its Mecca, Palestine its Jerusalem, France its Lourdes, and Italy its Loretto, but America's only shrines are her altars of patriotism." The Association for the Preservation of Virginia Antiquities will take your students to 1607 Jamestown by way of the Jamestown Rediscovery archaeological project, a ten-year, ongoing, interdisciplinary endeavor. Feel free to wander through the 22.5-acre site and see what has been found and how the excavation is being conducted. Objects such as coins, ceramics, tobacco pipes and cloth seals, weapons, and armor, including the 24-pound "pikeman's suit," reveal detailed facts about everyday life in the old outpost, where people dined primarily on turtles and fish as well as the occasional raccoon and one dead horse. The history of Jamestown includes profiles of Captain John Smith, Pocahontas, and John Rolfe in visual and textual detail that brings them to life.

Lewis and Clark Expedition

http://www.vpds.wsu.edu/WAHistCult/trail.html

Join students from the Virtual Professional Development School at Washington State University as they explore the states of Washington, Idaho, and Montana with Lewis and Clark. Each of the explorers' daily journal entries, which have been rewritten into contemporary English, can be retrieved from either a daily calendar or a map of their route.

Teachers will appreciate the activity suggestions (keyed to each of the journal entries), which include such ideas as journal writing, placing local flora and cultural artifacts on maps, and discussing (or second guessing) some of the explorers' decisions.

Louisiana Purchase

See Chapter 3—United States—Louisiana—New Orleans.

Louisiana State Museum

http://www.crt.state.la.us/crt/museum/lsmnet3.htm

Louisiana State Museum, established in 1911, is dedicated to preserving the state's culture and heritage. Exhibits include a history of Louisiana's extraordinary number of ethnic groups from colonization to reconstruction. As early nineteenth-century traveler William Darby remarked, "No city perhaps on the globe with an equal number of human beings presents a greater contrast of natural manners, language, and complexion than does New Orleans." The extensive exhibit on maps, with more than 100 cartographic artifacts and works of art, presents maps as "pictures of the world reflecting a people's cultural believes and perceptions." Using the maps and accompanying texts, student are able to study such topics as the cartographic rule of ethnocentricity, maps as political instruments, cultural assumptions, history, art, and even plagiarism. For example, the "War of Maps" waged between England and France during the first half of the eighteenth century shows how maps were used by competing powers to claim territories in the New World. This "cartographic confrontation" climaxed with the French and Indian War. Other sections of the exhibit focus on Louisiana's aviation history and evening wear from 1896 to 1996.

For other information contained in this site, see also Chapter 2—New Orleans Historic Buildings *and* Chapter 6—Art Museums *and* Fashion and Design.

Museum of New York

See also U.S. History—Nineteenth-Century Industry.

http://www.mcny.org

The Museum of New York chronicles the history, people, and events that have shaped New York City from its origins in 1898 to modern times. The online exhibitions feature narratives, photographs, research files, paintings, examples of the decorative arts, postcards, manuscripts, and other materials from the institution's collections. Past features have included chronicles of New York's ethnic parades, a celebration of the George and Ira Gershwin centennial, a history of Broadway, and design drawings from the 1939 World's Fair. Students will learn that the first circus performed on Broadway in 1793 was the origin of the word "jumbo." The featured elephant was so large and popular that a brand-new word was coined in his honor. Each week, there's a different *Bite of the Apple,* a brief photo or painting of an aspect of the city with a short narrative.

Nineteenth-Century Industry

http://bhw.buffnet.net

The Buffalo and Erie County Historical Society welcomes you to nineteenth-century Buffalo, New York. Visit the exhibit on Buffalo's *Grain District* for a detailed history of the grain industry, the impact of the Erie Canal, and Joseph Dart's invention of the grain elevator, which he describes as "substituting modern ingenuity for the backs of Irishmen." The tour also includes an interesting historical perspective on the times as told by *The Scoopers,* whose lives were characterized by irregular employment, low wages, and the saloon-based system of management. The second tour, *Fast Tracks*, which includes a tour of Central Terminal, describes the impact of the railroad on society and tells the story of the rise and fall of train depots. During the tour, your students may want to watch Presidents Abraham Lincoln, William McKinley and Theodore Roosevelt, who are visiting the city.

PBS American Experience Series

http://www.pbs.org/wgbh/pages/amex/

This site includes many photographs, anecdotes, and taped interviews from and overviews of each of the more than 25 programs featured in PBS's *The American Experience* series. The topics, which include study guides and reading lists, cover aspects of U.S. culture and history as diverse as the Donner Party; Hawaii's last queen; the orphan trains that shipped 10,000 homeless children in New York City to rural areas in the 1880s; the Cold War and the infamous U-2 CIA spy plane; crime and punishment; eighteenth-century midwifery; and the impact of inventions such as the telephone, television, Frisbee, and can opener on American society. Known for its intimate, intriguing details, interesting anecdotes and photographs, and unique perspective, *The American Experience* looks at events and people in the context of their times. Your students won't just meet people like Orson Welles, the Wright brothers, William Randolph Hearst, Andrew Carnegie, reporter and world traveler Nellie Bly, every twentieth-century U.S. president, and Carl Fisher (the man responsible for the founding of Miami Beach)—they will also learn how these people and the times shaped each other. Take your students across the country and back and forth through time from the Alaska gold rush to the Dust Bowl, from the building of the transcontinental railroad to the construction of the New York City subway, from the deadly influenza epidemic of 1918 to the beaches of Normandy and the Vietnam War.

Salem Witch Trials

http://www.nationalgeographic.com/features/97/salem

If you knew your life would be spared, would you confess to witchery or turn in a friend? Students will have to make this decision in *National Geographic*'s simulated version of sixteenth-century Salem. There is an excellent background on the Puritan inquisition that resulted in the loss of

25 lives and the imprisonment of innocent people. The dark graphics, the grim photographs, and the confused and terrified thoughts of the accused person—you—make for a harrowing journey not suited for younger children. At your trial, you have to decide whether to confess, even though you know you are innocent . . . or are you? So much has happened to you that it's difficult to know what's real. Learn how the hysteria of three 12-year-old girls was able to affect the lives of so many people. Other sections of the site include questions and answers from the resident historian of Salem. Students can also e-mail their own questions as well as participate in a forum in which people of all ages share their thoughts about the Salem experience. Be sure to send an e-mail postcard from sixteenth-century Salem to those unable to join you on your tour.

Texas

http://www.lsjunction.com

This site is administered by Lone Star Junction, a nonprofit organization established to preserve Texas history. This comprehensive site includes photographs of landscapes and local denizens such as the Texas horned lizard, coyote, roadrunner, and armadillo; a searchable database of over 10,000 Texans; online editions of rare and classic books about Texas; and famous documents such as the state constitution and William Barret Travis's appeal from the Alamo. While visiting the historic republic, you can listen to classic Texan and western songs. Be sure to visit the first state fair (May 1852). There's quite a bit to see so you may want to have an ample supply of skinplasters (currency). The more adventuresome may want to spend some time with the Texas Rangers or visit the five missions of Old San Antonio, including the Alamo.

Underground Railroad

See also Chapter 3—United States—New York—Pocantico Hills School—Sleepy Hollow, New York.

http://www.cr.nps.gov

The National Register of Historic Places provides this tour of 34 places that were a part of the Underground Railroad. There is a map of the most common escape routes, a background on the era, and descriptions and photographs of places such as the John Brown cabin in Kansas and the home of the Reverend George B. Hitchcock in Iowa—a safehouse for runaway slaves and abolitionists.

For other information contained in this site, see Women's History—National Register of Historic Places.

Vermont—Fort Ethan Allen

http://personalweb.smcvt.edu/thefort

Take a trip to Fort Ethan Allen in Vermont, courtesy of a student at St. Michael's College. The Fort, constructed in 1894, was home to soldiers and their families from the days of the Indian Wars to the Korean War. Be sure to pay a visit to the Buffalo Soldiers—African American cavalrymen sent to the Fort for a rest after their efforts in the Indian Wars. The Buffalo Soldiers were given their name by Native Americans who were impressed by their thick, curly hair and fighting skills. A collection of reminiscences by former inhabitants of the Fort include those of 12-year-old Pearl Milisci, who observed someone murdered during a drunken brawl.

WOMEN'S HISTORY

See also Chapter 1—Military History—World War II—Women's Air Force Service Pilots

National Register of Historic Places

http://www.cr.nps.gov

The National Register of Historic Places will take your students on a tour of New York and Massachusetts to honor the women who have shaped our nation's history. There are interactive maps, descriptions of the significance of each building, photographs, essays, and so on. The achievements of women in the fields of education, government, medicine, arts, commerce, women's suffrage, and the civil rights movement are covered as part of the National Register's *Discover Our Shared Heritage* travel series. In addition to the more well-known women such as Susan B. Anthony and Edith Wharton, students will have the opportunity to learn about such people as Madame C. J. Walker, America's first African American female millionaire, and astronomer, professor, and women's education crusader Maria Mitchell.

For other information contained in this site, see U.S. History—Underground Railroad.

A Celebration of Women Writers

http://www.cs.cmu.edu/afs/cs.cmu.edu/user/mmbt/www/women/writers.html

Professor Mary Mark Ockerbloom of Carnegie Mellon University invites students to visit women writers from 3,000 B.C. to the twentieth century. Stop by and see Kassiane, a Byzantine nun who wrote dozens of hymns. The site, arranged alphabetically, by century or by country, includes portraits, biographies, and samples of writing. Women who weren't primarily known as writers are also featured, including Abigail Adams and Bella Abzug. Whether you're looking for someone famous or trying to discover someone you haven't heard of, such as Muslim poet Shahnaz A'lami, you'll be surprised at the amount of influential women's writing that has always existed around the world.

CHAPTER 2

ARCHITECTURAL TOURS

These architectural tours are hosted by priests, architects, and even second graders. The tours range from the most primitive dwellings of the earliest civilizations to a modern-day energy-efficient house constructed from natural materials and cover everything from the earliest architectural drawings to modern AutoCAD techniques.

ALTERNATIVE ARCHITECTURE

Bini's Concrete Structures

http://www.binisystems.com

Italian architect Dante Bini will show you some of his patented architectural and construction methodology. Bini specializes in low-cost concrete buildings and structures, many of which can be constructed in 30 to 120 minutes. There are photographs, videos, and graphics along with descriptions of his buildings and explanations of his process.

Earthships

http://www.slip.net/~ckent/earthship

Hosts of this site wish to point out that "if you're looking for aliens or UFOs, you've come to the wrong place." *Earthships* are structures built from recyclable materials such as tires and aluminum cans. Students can view various structures while learning ecology by exploring such ideas as passive solar design, thermal mass, and renewable energy. Administrators of this site claim that these structures remain at a temperature of 60 to 70 degrees throughout the year without the use of auxiliary heating and cooling.

Natural Buildings

http://www.zianet.com/blackrange/br_pages/home.html

Natural Building Resources is an umbrella organization created to coordinate activities involving natural materials, sustainable architecture, and ecological principles. Visitors to this site can learn about constructing buildings out of straw bales, cobs, adobe, and bamboo and see actual structures in various stages of construction.

Solar House

http://solstice.crest.org/renewables/wlord/index.html
http://www.solarhouse.com

The Center for Renewable Energy and Sustainable Technology invites your class to follow the construction of a 2,900-square-foot solar house in Maine from site selection through completion. The tour includes explanations of solar heating (both solar thermal heat for hot water and photovoltaic for electricity) and solar power. A $6.57 electric bill in August isn't too bad, and in winter, the colder it becomes, the clearer the sky, so it's ideal for solar energy harvesting.

AMERICAN ARCHITECTURE

See also Chapter 3—United States—Washington, D.C.—Lincoln Memorial.

Tour 1

http://www.bc.edu/bc_org/avp/cas/fnart/fa267

Jeffrey Howe of Boston University has collected more than 750 digitized images of American architecture along with explanatory materials. This site illustrates the development of architecture in the United States from the seventeenth century to present times, with emphasis placed on architectural monuments. Howe also includes a section on skyscrapers, with charts, texts and photographs of America's tallest buildings, as well as the world's current tallest skyscraper in Kuala Lumpur. In this exceptionally well-organized site, information is arranged by date, style, purpose, location, and architect.

For other materials available at this site, see Chapter 2—European Architecture.

Tour 2

http://lcweb2.loc.gov/detroit/archamer.html

The Library of Congress exhibit *State Houses to Skyscrapers* documents significant architectural achievements from the eighteenth century. The tour, primarily comprising photographs from the Detroit Publishing Company Collection, is divided into *Capitol Buildings, Private Residences,* and *Skyscrapers,* and includes information on several architects. Students will be able to meet such notables as Charles Bulfinch, the first American-born professional architect; Thomas Jefferson; Benjamin Henry Latrobe; the team of William Holabird and Martin Root; and Gridley J. F. Bryant, who achieved his greatest success designing asylums.

ARCHIMEDIA PROJECT
http://www-lib.haifa.ac.il/www/art/archimedia.html

The Archimedia Project, hosted by the University of Haifa Library, concentrates on the architecture of Ancient Egypt and Mesopotamia. Students will be able to learn how ancient structures such as the pyramids, ziggurats, and the Palace of Nestor in Pylos were constructed by studying various views, sections, plans, and axonometric and computerized reconstructions. There are also brief narrative descriptions of each structure that tell us, for example, that the Cheops Pyramid in Giza was the tallest pyramid ever built at 479 feet in height and contained 3.4 million cubic yards of stone. (Ironically, the only surviving replica of Cheops himself is about 2 inches high.)

ARCHITECTURE THROUGH THE AGES
http://library.advanced.org/10098/index.html

This tour, created by 14-year-olds, discusses and illustrates Aztec, Mayan, Greek, Roman, Chinese, classical, cathedral, and Egyptian architecture and how it reflected and shaped various societies. The section on Roman architecture includes the Colosseum, the Forum of Caesar, the 300,000-seat Circus Maximus, the Pantheon, the Temples of the Forum Boarium, the Arch of Titus, and a typical Roman home. There are also virtual tours of the National Cathedral in Washington, D.C., the Great Wall of China, and Egypt, which are movies and require a rather long time to download.

AUTOCAD MODELING
http://www.princeton.edu/~asce/const_95/const.html

Professor Ahmet Cakmak of Princeton University's Department of Civil Engineering and Operations Resources and his students have constructed 3-D structural models of some of Istanbul's oldest buildings as well as the wall of the city. Working from photos and blueprints and using AutoCAD drafting software, they have analyzed Istanbul's ancient architecture to determine the buildings' susceptibility to earthquake damage. The model constructed by his class will eventually include a full topographical and structural model of ancient Constantinople, but in the meantime, students visiting the site are able to gain insight into the uses of AutoCAD drafting software as well as an appreciation of the aesthetics, mechanics, and wisdom of ancient architects.

BAUHAUS SCHOOL OF ARCHITECTURE
http://craton.geol.BrockU.CA/guest/jurgen/bauhaus.htm

In 1919, Walter Gropius was appointed to head a new institution in Weimar, Germany, called the Bauhaus. Gropius's goal was to bring the arts and architecture together into a single discipline. The movement attracted people from all over the world, including Ludwig Mies van der Rohe and Paul Klee. Your students can learn about this period in architecture as well as gain a historical perspective on the politics and culture of the times. There are drawings, photographs, site plans, murals, and information about Gropius and other Bauhaus figures.

CASTLES AND CATHEDRALS

See also Chapter 2—European Architecture *and* Gargoyles.

Amiens Cathedral
http://www.arch.columbia.edu/DDL/projects/amiens/index.html

Columbia University's Digital Design Lab, in collaboration with the Art History Department, takes students from the blueprints to the spiritual and architectural glory of Paris's Amiens Cathedral. Using computer-generated graphics and photographs to construct the audiovisual tour, the Digital Lab examines the mid-1800s physical reconstruction of the Gothic cathedral and provides a detailed text explaining the Christian symbolism of the design and artwork. Students will learn such facts as why Mary is larger than Christ, the role of the prophets, and how the cathedral's design incorporates the central theme of duality in Christian religion. The tour, for upper level students, includes videos and music.

Durham Cathedral and Castle
http://www.dur.ac.uk/~diaOwww/c_tour/tour.html

The Durham Cathedral and Castle is one of the finest examples of the Anglo-Norman school of architecture. Students at Durham University's Center for Law and Computing will take you on a tour of the building and describe and explain its architectural features and their historical significance. For example, the north door and sanctuary knocker is symbolic of the right of sanctuary granted to all criminals during the twelfth century. A criminal used the knocker to catch the attention of watchmen, who allowed entry to the sanctuary. The person was granted monastery protection for 40 days, during which time he had to choose between trial and voluntary exile.

Lviv Architecture

http://www.interlog.com/~alepki/lviv/lviv.htm

Lviv is one of the oldest settlements in the Ukraine—dating back to 1256. This tour examines significant buildings spanning Old Rus to Art Nouveau architecture. Sites include such significant structures as St. Nicholas Church (the oldest architectural monument in Lviv, dating back to the thirteenth century), the Chapel of Boims (an example of Renaissance architecture), and the Kornyakt Tower. Your students will even be allowed entrance to the Armenian Cathedral, which is usually closed to the public. The cathedral houses approximately 3,000 historical artifacts that include 2,000 icons.

Medieval Castles

http://www.isle-of-man.com/heritage/sites/peel-castle/index.htm

Travel back in time to Peel Castle in St. Patrick's Isle in the Irish Sea to experience life in a medieval castle. The room-by-room tour begins with a panoramic view of the castle from a bluff at the edge of the sea. Through textual or audio narration, students will find out about the advantages and disadvantages of such things as the "toilet system." Although conveniently located near the outer wall for efficient drainage and olfactory reasons, the system, in the words of the author, "also provided a means of entry into the castle for a determined enemy." Judging from an excavation of the castle graveyard, the people had surprisingly few broken bones, yet numerous spinal injuries—probably from lifting heavy loads. The big problems, however, were gum disease, tooth decay, and abscessed teeth.

Monuments of Georgia (Eastern Europe)

http://www.parliament.ge/georgia/culture/ancient/mon.html

The Georgian parliament hosts this historical tour of Georgian monuments. Most of the sites are cathedrals, churches, temples, and monasteries dating from the fifth through fourteenth centuries. There are photographs and historical and architectural narrative overviews.

Sistine Chapel

See Chapter 1—Renaissance.

CHATEAU DE VERSAILLES

See Chapter 1—French History.

CHICAGO CULTURAL CENTER
http://www.ci.chi.il.us/Tourism/CultureCenterTour

The building that now houses the Chicago Cultural Center was constructed in 1897 as the city's first permanent library. Students can tour the Beaux Arts–style facility, which features rooms modeled after the Doge's Palace in Venice, the Palazzo Vecchio in Florence, and the Acropolis in Athens. The tour focuses on both the large scale and intricate detail. After the tour, students can stop outside and go on a virtual tour of Chicago.

COLUMBIAN EXPOSITION
See Chapter 1—Columbian Exposition—1893.

EUROPEAN ARCHITECTURE
See also Castles and Cathedrals.
http://www.bc.edu/bc_org/avp/cas/fnart/arch/contents_europe.html

Jeffrey Howe from Boston College will take you on a European architectural tour, starting with Stonehenge, which dates from prehistoric times. Howe has amassed an extensive collection of slides showing the Doric, Ionic, and Corinthian Greek orders; Romanesque and Gothic churches; medieval fortifications; fifteenth- and twentieth-century structures; and Belgian construction. The tour encompasses the most modern European architecture and also covers such familiar landmarks as the Eiffel Tower and the Chateau de Versailles, as well as ordinary houses and cottages dating back several centuries. The site is short on text, so be prepared to supplement this extensive visual tour with other materials.

For other materials contained in this site, see American Architecture.

FUNERARY ARCHITECTURE
See Chapter 3—United States—Illinois—Chicago's Graveyards.

GARGOYLES
http://ils.unc.edu/garg/garghp4.html

You meet gargoyles in the strangest places, as the students from the School of Information and Library Science at the University of North Carolina point out. These hideous-looking creatures, once carved into churches and cathedrals to frighten away evil spirits, are also found on other urban buildings, and now they are threatened by the evil spirits of urban renewal and pollution. Your students can see dozens of gargoyles and learn all about these strange creatures and the people and times that created them.

GAUDI, ANTONI
http://futures.wharton.upenn.edu/~jonath22/gaudi.html

Architect and designer Antoni Gaudi i Cornet's work in Barcelona led to some of the city's most notable landmarks. Jonathan Meltzer, a finance major at the Wharton School, wants to show your students the works by this Art Nouveau architect and designer. The tour includes houses, temples, and schools designed by Gaudi between 1883 and 1910. Students will see why Walter Gropius called Gaudi's work a "marvel of technical perfection" and can also find out what Salvador Dali, Le Corbusier, and George Orwell had to say.

ITALIAN VILLAS
http://www.boglewood.com/palladio/home.html

Eighteen villas designed by Renaissance architect Andrea Palladio survive in the Veneto area of Italy, near Venice. Palladio's structures revolutionized Western European architecture in the seventeenth and eighteenth centuries and produced the school of southern architecture in the nineteenth century. Tours and analyses of the villas and information about Palladio's life are available at this site.

NEW ORLEANS HISTORIC BUILDINGS
http://www.crt.state.la.us/crt/museum/lsmnet3.htm

The Louisiana State Museum in New Orleans is housed within eight historic landmark buildings that are available for your students to tour. The buildings, situated in New Orleans' French Quarter, represent many architectural styles. The Cabildo, the site of the Louisiana Purchase transfer, built in 1795–1799 as the seat of the Spanish municipal government, also once served as the home of the state supreme court. The Old U.S. Mint, designed by William Strickland in classical Greek Revival style, is the only building in the country to have served as both a U.S. and a Confederate mint. Other buildings include the 1839 Arsenal designed by James Dakin and associated with the Battle of Liberty Place; Madame John's eighteenth-century row houses that are an excellent example of Louisiana Creole eighteenth-century architecture; and the Jackson and Creole Houses, which are representative of New Orleans' antebellum period.

For other materials contained in this site, see Chapter 1—U.S. History—Louisiana State Museum.

PRAIRIE SCHOOL OF ARCHITECTURE
http://www.capecod.net/~gmiller/contents.htm

A visit to the "Airplane House" in Woods Hole, Massachusetts, a bungalow-style home designed by William Gray Purcell and George Grant Elmslie, provides a valuable educational resource for learning about the Prairie School of Architecture. The house was originally built in 1912 for $30,000. At the time, citizens petitioned to have the building razed and replaced with a more traditional structure. It is now considered one of the greatest homes in the United States. While touring the home, students can learn about Purcell, Elmslie, Louis Sullivan, and Frank Lloyd Wright's nine principles of prairie-style architecture. There is also a section on the tesseract—a geometrical formation that allows one to experience fourth-dimensional consciousness through the physical senses.

PRINCETON UNIVERSITY

See Chapter 3—United States—New Jersey.

ROMAN VILLA
http://www.dhm.de/museen/stein/stein_e.html

Pack your togas for this trip to a third-century Roman villa discovered in 1973 in Hechingen-Stein, Germany. Feel free to wander through the grounds and the villa's 20 rooms. If you choose to take the trip during the cold season, we suggest you stay inside the main rooms, which are equipped with a smoke-free floor heating system called a hypocaust. And don't miss the baths! Administrators will take you through the entire bathing ritual, from the changing room to the cold bath to the tepidarium (this is also where gymnastics takes place) to the hot baths, where you finally get to relax and socialize. Excavation is ongoing, and your students can read progress reports while learning about the actual process.

SKYSCRAPERS

See American Architecture.

CHAPTER 3

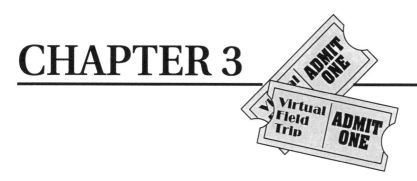

SEE THE WORLD

Travel the world from the comfort of your classroom. Visit with aborigines in Australia, celebrate holidays in China, take a ride on a giant tortoise in the Galapagos, check out the Holy Land, drop in on schools around the world, see all our national monuments and landmarks in a few hours, and learn how to send a surrogate stuffed animal out into the world and track his travels and souvenirs on the Internet. As they say in virtual travel, *Bon Viajes!*

AMAZONIA

See also Chapter 3—Brazil, Ecuadorian Rain Forest, *and* Worldwide Travel—Tour 3—United Nations.
http://www.tef-telecom.com/amazon

During the summer of 1997, Andrew Mercer, a computer programmer from ANZ Bank in New Zealand, embarked on a trip through the Amazon River system in Brazil and Peru. Mercer shares his encounters with the people, history, sights, plants, and animal life of the region through daily travel diaries, texts, and photographs. His descriptions and pictures of local animals range from the anteater and capybara (the world's largest rodent, which he describes as "an overgrown guinea pig about the same size as a dog") to the urubu, or black vulture. Pay attention to him before you wander off into the forest. It will be important to distinguish, for example, between the ordinary tree frog and the arrow poison frog, which is only 2–4 centimeters long yet has the most powerful venom produced by nature. (One ten-thousandth of a gram can kill a human.) He'll also tell you about life in the river, including over 2,000 species of river and jungle denizens from the anaconda to the piranha. Those more interested in social activities can spend some time with the local *caboclos*, gold miners and prospectors, Indian hunters, Incas, and rubber barons.

Suggested classroom activities use the information on-site and links to other resources to enable students to practice math, social studies, and research skills.

ARCTIC CIRCLE

See Chapter 5—The Animal Kingdom—Animals of the Arctic.

AUSTRALIA

See also Chapter 3—United States—New York—Greece Central School District.
http://ann-nt.altnews.com.au/twscairns/capeyork/tour/tour.htm

The Cape York Peninsula in northeast Australia is the largest expanse of high-quality wilderness on the continent, and it includes areas from arid grasslands to tropical rainforests. The Cape York Indigenous Environment Foundation, dedicated to preserving and protecting the land, the animals, the plants, and the aborigines, wants to take you on a tour. They'll show you the amazing biodiversity and tell you about the aboriginal history and culture. See one of the world's largest collections of sandstone rock art, dating back 30,000 years. The tour includes photos, movies, and sounds, and all the information is presented from a perspective of deep respect for the people and environment.

BASQUE REGION

http://students.washington.edu/~buber/Basque

Blas Uberuaga, a Basque computer expert born in Idaho and currently a computer scientist at Weber University, is the man to visit for anything you want to know about the Basque region and culture. In addition to information, graphics, and photographs concerning local folklore, art, culture, and geography, Uberuaga runs a chat room and bulletin board so that Basques and their friends around the world can keep in touch. Basques often send him current photographs of the region, which are available for viewing. And the recipes, such as *chipirones en su tinta* (squids in ink) are wonderful. Your students can even learn the Basque language. Much of the information is also available in French, Spanish, and, of course, Basque and English.

BRAZIL

See also Chapter3—Amazonia *and* Worldwide Travel—Tour 3.
http://pasture.ecn.purdue.edu/~agenhtml/agenmc/brazil/brazil.html

Students of Purdue University will take your students on a tour of Brazil. It's an ideal place for them to visit because more than 70 percent of the people are under the age of 30. Tour the Amazon rain forest and the cities of Sao Paulo and Rio de Janeiro, party at Carnival or other festivals, hang out with the local gauchos of the southern region, listen to local music, or try such local recipes as stewed pumpkin and deep-fried cassava.

CANADA

See Chapter 1—Native Americans—Virtual Keeping House: A First Nation's Gallery *and* Chapter 6—Art Museums—National Gallery of Canada.

CHINA, REPUBLIC OF

See also Chapter 2—Architecture Through the Ages.
http://www.gio.gov.tw/info/festival_c/index_e.htm

Celebrate year-round holidays in the Republic of China. The main holidays in Taiwan are divided into two categories—the traditional holidays associated with the lunar calendar and commemorative holidays keyed to the Western calendar. Students will be more interested in the former, which include New Years Eve, the Chinese New Year and Lantern Festival, Tomb Sweeping Day, the Dragon Boat Festival, and the Ghost Festival. By perusing descriptions of the holidays and their accompanying myths and colorful artwork, students will have a chance to learn about Chinese culture and how the lunar calendar works.

ECUADORIAN RAIN FOREST

http://www.eduweb.com/amazon.html

Explore the world of the Ecuadorian rain forest and the Quichua people through online games and activities. Students can try running a commercial eco-tourism project along the Rio Napo to learn about the area's physical and human geography as well as the risks and benefits of eco-tourism as an economic development strategy. Those who prefer the old way of life will also be confronted with decisions such as how much land to slash and burn, what crops to plant, and how to balance cash crops with conservation strategies.

EGYPT

See also Chapter 2—Architecture Through the Ages.
http://www.horus.ics.org.eg

Little Horus will take your students on a tour of Egypt, conducted in Arabic or English. He will also teach basic Arabic, share his recipes for traditional Egyptian food such as *ghorayeba* and *keshk*, play games and tell stories. Students will have an opportunity to learn about the Egyptian economy, culture, holidays, and history. Each month, Horus will take your students to see a different monument, such as the pyramids or the

Sphinx. His friend, Egyptian First Lady Suzanne Mubarak, is the head of an international charity for poor children, and she will take your students to visit some of them, show a video, and play one of their songs. Others may prefer to pay a visit to President Hosni Mubarak.

FRANCE
http://www.paris.org

The Paris Pages, a consortium of individuals and businesses, will take your students on an intimate tour of Paris, from the famous monuments to everyday bistro and coffee shops. All information is available in French and English, and site administrators invite French-language classes to submit photographs and information about themselves and their experiences in Paris, which can be presented on-site. Bring your class on this trip to learn the nitty-gritty details of *la ville lumière,*—coffee prices, current weather, menus, and maps.

GALAPAGOS ISLANDS
http://www.terraquest.com/galapagos

It's off to the Galapagos Islands, nature's evolutionary laboratory where Charles Darwin developed his theories of evolution. Each year a team of researchers, including some children, tours the islands and sends back both photographs, including stunning panoramic ones, and daily dispatch reports via the Internet. Because these photos and reports are archived, your students can either participate in the next virtual trip or view past material. They will love the multicolored iguanas, blue-footed boobies, unique vegetation, and giant sea turtles, which have flourished and survived because of the protection that the islands afford from natural predators. Twelve-year-old Tina followed the eco-tourist guidelines, which prohibit touching any animals but allowed her to stand still while they touched her, and a giant tortoise practically brushed against her. The dispatch team, which also fields your classes' e-mail queries, covers not only the biology and zoology but also the history of the islands from the first explorers, pirates, and navigators to Darwin's visit aboard the HMS Beagle.

GEORGIA (EASTERN EUROPE)
See Chapter 2—Castles and Cathedrals—Monuments of Georgia.

GREENLAND
See Chapter 3—Worldwide Travel—Tour 3.

ISRAEL

http://www.virtual.co.il/channels/israel/timetravel

Take a tour of Jerusalem from its ancient origins to modern times. Your tour guides will be King David, Herod the Great, Dirk the Crusader, Suleiman the Great, and Tammar—a current Jewish resident. The most important periods in the country's history are covered. What better way to learn than from those who actually took part in the events? The site uses video, audio, narratives, and photographs to relate history and show you the local sites. Remember, some of these people are going to be rather self-serving. Herod, for example, complains that history has painted him as a bad guy. Despite some of the things he may have done, he says, "I just about completely rebuilt the temple and it was one of the great wonders of the ancient world. I was King of Judea from 37 to 4 B.C.E. During that time I overhauled the whole city. It was a triumph of urban planning. I built parks, palaces, big theaters, marketplaces, fortified walls. . . ." Dirk the Crusader will take you back to the first Crusader kingdom, which lasted from 1099 to 1187 C.E. His tour begins at Herod's Gate, where he'll tell you how the crusaders, led by Godfrey of Bouillon, conquered Jerusalem. During the tour, students will visit every holy Jewish, Christian, and Moslem site in the city. If you become tired of history, spend some time with Tammar, who will tell you about modern-day Israel. She'll take you to the Western Wall, the southern Temple Mount excavations, the Jewish Quarter, the Hurva Synagogue, and Lion's Gate.

ITALY

See Chapter 2—Italian Villas.

JAPAN

http://www.us-japan.org/edomatsu

The Japan-America Society of the state of Washington welcomes you to Edo, the ancient name for Tokyo. For most Japanese people, Edo represents everything about Japanese traditional culture. As you enter the large gate that marks the last of the *seki* (barriers) into Edo, you will be carefully checked by the guards for swords and other weapons. Edo is a peaceful place, and only samurais are allowed to carry weapons. The tour is then presented in the form of an interactive story that allows students to learn about the buildings, people, culture, fashion, and cuisine of Edo.

MADAGASCAR

See Chapter 3—Worldwide Travel—Tour 4.

NAMIBIA

See Chapter 3—Worldwide Travel—Tour 4.

PERU

See Chapter 3—Amazonia.

SPAIN

See Chapter 2—Gaudi, Antoni.

TRAVEL BUDDIES
http://www.greeceny.com/projects.htm

Perhaps the next best thing to a virtual worldwide field trip is to follow a friend's journey. The Greece Central School District in New York tells you how to set up a "Travel Buddies" program and send your own little pal around the world to other schools. Follow the worldwide travels of Willie the Wandering Wallaby. Each school he visits takes him on a local field trip or to someone's home, and many contribute items to his duffle-bag and post reports on the Internet. So far, Willie has been to Mississippi's d'Iberville Elementary and Middle Schools (he arrived too late for Mardi Gras, but the kids gave him some doubloons, photographs, and a video-tape); a Bristol, England, primary school where he met some Welsh birds of prey and went to a sheep farm (he helped deliver lambs, "participated in mucking, and the whole shebang") ; and a Glenview elementary school in Prince George, British Columbia, where he met Mr. P. G. (a statue that welcomes visitors to the city). Be sure to have a talk with your travel buddy before he or she embarks on the journey. P. J. McMossey from Gillette, Wyoming, got in a bit of trouble in Maryland. Apparently he tried to sneak on to one of the National Guard trucks during a field trip and got caught by the police. Luckily, he had his identification and was very brave, so they gave him a ride back to the Cromwell school.

For other information contained in this site, see Chapter 3—United States—New York—Greece Central School District.

UKRAINE

See Chapter 2—Castles and Cathedrals—Lviv Architecture.

UNITED STATES

See also Chapter 1—U.S. History.

Central Intelligence Agency

http://www.odci.gov/cia/ciakids

The Central Intelligence Agency (CIA) has a special tour for your students, during which agents will share their knowledge of history, geography, and the people and animals that are instrumental in America's national security. Step back in time and meet some of the people involved in intelligence, such as James Armistead Lafayette, a Virginia slave who spied for George Washington; Morris "Moe" Berg, intelligence officer, linguist, lawyer, and baseball player; General William "Wild Bill" Donovan, known as the father of U.S. intelligence; and Virginia Hill, the only female civilian to receive the Distinguished Service Cross. Even Benjamin Franklin was involved! Stop by the *Exhibit Center* where some of the artifacts representative of the history of U.S. intelligence, such as the microdot camera, the silver dollar hollow container, and CIA-produced pamphlets, are displayed. In order to successfully carry out their mission, personnel must be well schooled in geography. They will share some of their knowledge of the world with you, including information from the CIA *World Fact Book,* and tell you about the intelligence cycle and the checks and balances imposed on the organization by the president and Congress. Students can even try on a disguise! Even with all the technology available, the CIA still relies on help from such animals as Bogart of the canine corps. Bo is retired and now conducts tours, during which he will introduce you to his buddies and show you how they are trained. Harry Recon—ace photo pigeon—will tell you about the role played by aerial photography pigeons and show you some of the pictures he and his pals have taken.

The Great American Landmark Adventure

http://www.cr.nps.gov

This tour, conducted by the National Park Service in conjunction with the History Channel and the American Architectural Foundation, takes your students on a 3,000-year journey via U.S. landmarks—from prehistoric caves to the first rocket to the moon. Each landmark visit begins with a black-and-white drawing by Roxie Monro, which students may print and color. Be sure to submit your work because some of the best will be displayed on-site. Students will learn what a landmark is, how it is chosen, who owns it, and who takes care of it. The site also has a teacher's guide with activities for relating each landmark to current events, science, art, social studies, and other curricular areas. Diverse sites include the Eastern State Penitentiary in Philadelphia, Pennsylvania, which was a model prison in 1829; Independence Rock in Casper, Wyoming, a resting place for travelers on the Oregon Trail (some of the names that they painted or carved onto the rock are still visible); and the Boston Public Garden.

UNITED STATES—ALASKA

See also Chapter 5—The Animal Kingdom—Animals of the Arctic.

Anne Hopkins Wein Elementary School

http://www3.northstar.k12.ak.us/schools/awe/awe.html

Are you a sourdough (knowledgeable about Alaska) or a cheechako (green, but full of enthusiasm)? Find out from the students at the K–5 Anne Hopkins Wein Elementary School in Fairbanks. By the time students finish sharing interesting Alaskan facts and "mounds of moose megabytes," you are sure to become a bona fide cheechako. Learn why moose, almost as prevalent as students in the Fairbanks area, "look so goofy," what they eat (they love willow but hate spruce), how to get along with them, and how they protect themselves. There is even information on and photographs of moose products, ranging from clothing and artwork to "shish-ka-poops," made from moose droppings. Students can also read the daily newspaper (three people drowned last spring after running into the water to escape bears) and check the current weather.

UNITED STATES—CALIFORNIA

Cabrillo National Monument

http://www.nps.gov/cabr

Juan Rodriguez Cabrillo, often overshadowed by Hernán Cortez (with whom he served in battles against the Aztecs), entered San Diego Bay on September 28, 1552. He was the first European to set foot on what later became the west coast of the United States, and in 1913, President Woodrow Wilson authorized the Cabrillo National Monument. The site presents an excellent historical overview of the famous explorer and shares some little-known facts. Your students will learn that it was smallpox rather than the warriors who determined the outcome of this battle as well as the expansion of the Spanish empire. While you are there, be sure to stop in at the Old Point Loma lighthouse, learn about the local gray whale migration, the military history of San Diego Bay, and tidepools.

Fort McArthur Museum

http://www.ftmac.org/fmmhp.htm

This museum, located in San Pedro, California, is dedicated to the preservation and interpretation of the history of Fort McArthur, a United States army post that guarded the Los Angeles harbor from 1914 to 1974. History buffs will be impressed by the extensive information available about General Douglas McArthur and his father, after whom the fort was named. There are also blueprints, armaments, and Nike missile displays available for viewing.

Joe Nightingale School

http://orcutts1.sbceo.k12.ca.us/public/nightingale

Welcome to Joe Nightingale School's student-created home page. The students are quite proud of the Santa Maria, California, region where they live and will take you on a tour of the local sites—past and present. Third graders will tell you all about the Chumash Indians, and the fourth graders will take you on a tour of local missions. Fifth graders will tell you all about local ocean and marine life, including clown and puff fish, sharks, whales, dolphins, otters, seals, and kelp, which fifth grader Crystal says can grow up to 1½ feet per day. Or simply wander around Santa Maria with some of the students. They will introduce you to their friend, the purple lady, and, if you go to the *Purple Stuff* page, you can peregrinate through her preposterous purplish life.

Nike Missile Site

http://www.nikemissile.org

Remember when missile sites were actually located inside metropolitan areas, and schools held air raid drills? The U.S. National Park Service will take your students on a tour of an inoperative Nike missile site in San Francisco. The tour includes lessons about military history and several short videos, including the Hercules launch and lives of the crew. There are also links to other inoperative U.S. missile sites and reminiscences by veterans.

Queen Mary

http://www.queenmary.org

And your students think the *Titanic* was big? Take them to see the *Queen Mary* in Long Beach, California, where they can compare the two. (The *Queen Mary* is 140 feet longer.) Among the historical and social information that might interest your class is that third-class passengers were allowed to use the pool for brief periods in the afternoon, but the water was changed before first-class passengers returned.

UNITED STATES—COLORADO

See Chapter 1—U.S. History—American West—Colorado Lore, Legend, and Fact.

UNITED STATES—FLORIDA

Miami Beach

See Chapter 1—U.S. History—PBS American Experience Series.

UNITED STATES—GEORGIA

See Chapter 1—U.S. History—Georgia.

UNITED STATES—HAWAII

See Chapter 1—U.S. History—PBS American Experience Series.

UNITED STATES—ILLINOIS

Chicago Cultural Center

See Chapter 2—Chicago Cultural Center.

Chicago's Graveyards

http://www.graveyards.com

Graveyards are an overlooked source of education about history and architecture. Tours available at this site include Chicago's famous Graceland Cemetery, where students will be able to learn about such historical figures as George Pullman, Louis Sullivan, Potter Palmer, John Peter Altgeld, Daniel Burnham, Marshall Field, and Allan Pinkerton—the world's first private detective and first head of the U.S. Secret Service. Rosehill Cemetery, noted for its Civil War reenactments, offers valuable information about Civil War soldiers and other notables. Some of the best funerary art and architecture can be found at Bohemian National Cemetery, where students can learn about Chicago's former mayor, Anton Cermak. Other mayors such as Harold Washington and William Hale Thompson are at Oakwoods, along with Enrico Fermi and Olympian Jesse Owens. Or you may prefer to stop by St. Henry's Cemetery to visit the grave of Henry Muno, one of the most famous faces in the nation—he's on every box of Cracker Jacks.

Columbian Exposition

See Chapter 1—Columbian Exposition—1893.

Twin Groves Junior High

See Chapter 1—Renaissance.

UNITED STATES—INDIANA

Loocootee Elementary School—Indiana
http://www.siec.k12.in.us/~west/proj/index.html

This school does an outstanding job of integrating the Internet with its curriculum. Students begin using the Internet in the primary grades. Instead of the participating in the standard "100th day" activities, for example, these students found sites that had something to do with 100, such as a site with a picture of a 100 dollar bill and one that displayed 100 jelly beans. Other students collected 100 e-mail messages from around the world. Mrs. Patton's first-grade class won the grand prize on Microsoft's Encarta Website for their Abraham Lincoln project, providing a quiz, an Internet treasure hunt, photographs of pioneer life, and other activities. The students are kind enough to give clues to the answers, and they are really polite if you are wrong. Other classes have done projects on hedgehogs, the months of the year, and the three little pigs. Be sure to take your students on the North American scavenger hunt. They will be applying for jobs as tour guides, and it's their responsibility to learn all they can about the continent's geography, environment, history, holidays, and customs. This is accomplished by following links to Websites (provided by Loocootee students) that contain information for completing tests and activities.

UNITED STATES—LOUISIANA

See also Chapter 1—U.S. History—Louisiana State Museum; Chapter 2—New Orleans Historic Buildings; *and* Chapter 6—Art Museums—Louisiana State Museum *and* Fashion and Design—Louisiana State Museum.

New Orleans
http://www.gatewayno.com/index.html

Start at the corner of Bourbon and Royal for a fun- and fact-filled trip through the Big Easy. History buffs may choose to travel back in time to learn about the Louisiana Purchase and the War of 1812 or to meet such notables as Jean Lafitte, Walker Percy, Truman Capote, or Tennessee Williams. Be sure to collect some New Orleans recipes while you are there. The locals will tell you all about andouille and beignets and even show you how to make a roux. You will also learn the difference between Creole and Cajun cooking. All of the musical greats are sure to be in town while you are on a virtual field trip. Stop by to meet and hear artists such as Louis Armstrong, Sidney Bechet, Fats Domino (who has sold more records than Elvis Presley or the Beatles), Jelly Roll Morton, Joe "King" Oliver (his Creole Jazz Band was the first black ensemble to be recorded), and the members of the Marsalis family. Of course, you won't want to miss Mardi Gras or the Vieux Carré. Have a great time and *laissez le bon temps rouler!*

UNITED STATES—MARYLAND

North Hagerstown High School—Maryland

http://www.fred.net/nhhs/nhhs.html

Students in North Hagerstown have been busy learning about government, U.S. history, and the civil rights movement. The ninth-grade class civil rights project is exceptionally impressive. There are interactive sections, including a Dr. Martin Luther King Jr. trivia game, black history quizzes on Harriet Tubman and Frederick Douglass, online debates, timelines, a newspaper, short stories, and essays.

UNITED STATES—MINNESOTA

See Chapter 1—Maritime History—Minnesota Historical Society.

UNITED STATES—NEW HAMPSHIRE

http://www.portsmouthnh.com/harbourtrail/index.htm

Follow the Harbour Trail through the city of Portsmouth as it passes more than 70 scenic and historical points of interest, including ten buildings listed in the National Register of Historic Places. It's quite a long tour, stretching over 350 years from Portsmouth's beginning in 1623, when it was originally named Strawberry Banke, to modern times. Sites include the Portsmouth Naval Shipyard (where the 1905 Treaty of Portsmouth ended the Russo-Japanese War), the John Paul Jones house (also the house featured in many commercials for Sears paint), and the USS Albacore, one of the United States' first submarines.

UNITED STATES—NEW JERSEY

Princeton University

http://www.princeton.edu/~okkey/index.html

Princeton University students will take you on a tour of their campus. Undergraduate students, who have volunteered their time and expertise for these tours since 1935, have recently created this virtual tour with photographs, narratives, movies, and audio. Be sure to stop at the Gothic-style University Chapel, which seats more than 2,000 people on pews made from army surplus wood originally designed for Civil War gun carriages. Other sites include Nassau Hall, which survived bombardment during the American Revolution (a cannonball scar is still visible), an Italianate mansion built in 1849, gardens, and the university's male and female tiger sculptures that were erected in 1969 to commemorate the arrival of women at the university.

UNITED STATES—NEW MEXICO

The Great Kiva Tour

http://www.sscf.ucsb.edu/anth/projects/great.kiva/elite/imtour.html

Anthropologist John Kantner will take your class to a genuine kiva, an ancient ceremonial lodge used by the ancestral Puebloans and their contemporary Pueblo descendants for at least 1,000 years. One archaeologist has called the Chetro Ketl Great Kiva, located in Chiaco Canyon in the San Juan basin of New Mexico, "the most remarkable structure in the Southwest." The tour begins at the top of the stairs, after visitors receive permission from the clan member guarding the entrance. "Come in," says the kiva priest. "Bring joy and health to the people! Come to regenerate the Earth, procreate and germinate the corn, the soil, the waters, and our women." Once permission to enter is granted, students may wander about at their leisure, viewing the numerous artifacts and petroglyphs. If they get lost, an overall floor plan will show them the way. Occasionally students can also watch movie clips and hear Hopi ceremonial songs.

UNITED STATES—NEW YORK

See also Chapter 1—U.S. History—Museum of New York.

Brooklyn Botanic Garden

See Chapter 5—Arboretums and Botanic Gardens.

Buffalo Grain District and Railroads

See Chapter 1—U.S. History—Nineteenth-Century Industry.

Greece Central School District

http://www.greeceny.com/projects.htm

Students and teachers throughout the district have been busy making Web pages to show their work. If you are looking for ways to incorporate the Internet into your curriculum, pay a visit to this New York state school district. There is an art gallery displaying the works of K–12 students, photographs of the student-made Iroquois village longhouse models, reports on books written by Tomie de Paola and Gary Paulsen, and trips to Queensland, Australia. The *West Ridge Peace Builders* have created a "peaceable school," where all teachers and students are directly involved in conflict resolution. The K–3 students use literature, games, and discussions, and the fourth and fifth graders have established a system of peer mediation. There are lists of applicable books, peace logos designed by students, illustrated interactive stories on mediation written by the kids (at each step you can choose whether you want to escalate or de-escalate the situation), and links to other world wide web sites dealing with peace and conflict resolution.

See also Chapter 3—Travel Buddies.

Pocantico Hills School—Sleepy Hollow, New York

http://www2.lhric.org/pocantico.html

The students and staff at Pocantico Elementary School have won several awards for their school project on Harriet Tubman and the Underground Railroad. The second graders have developed this site, which includes a timeline, a quiz, character sketches, crossword puzzles, maps of the Underground Railroad, photographs, and links to further information. We learned about the "Drinking Gourd"—a coded song used to communicate the route for an escape from Alabama to Mississippi. Other grades have also contributed to the site. The third and fourth graders have developed an *Encyclopedia of Women,* which covers people from Madeleine Albright to Laura Ingalls Wilder, and fourth graders will share their essays about the United States and Latin America.

For other information on the Underground Railroad, see Chapter 1—U.S. History—Underground Railroad.

United Nations

http://www.pbs.org/tal/un

This tour, sponsored by the Public Broadcasting Service and Turner Communications, concentrates on the structure and purpose of the United Nations (UN). The tour includes photographs and descriptions of the UN headquarters building's key assembly rooms, unique works of art such as Foucault's pendulum and the stained-glass window designed by artist Marc Chagall, and the Dag Hammarskjöld Library. The complete texts of important documents such as the UN Charter, the Statute of the International Court of Justice, and the Universal Declaration of Human Rights are also available. Teachers should check out the classroom activities, which include a teacher resource book and lesson plans such as the five steps of negotiation and mediation.

UNITED STATES—NORTH CAROLINA

Duke University

See Chapter 2—Gargoyles.

UNITED STATES—TEXAS

See Chapter 1—U.S. History—Texas.

UNITED STATES—VIRGINIA

Oak View Elementary School—Fairfax, Virginia

http://oakview.fcps.edu

We were amazed when we looked at *Stuff Done Here* at Oak View Elementary school (K–6). It seems that every class has been involved in activities—from the sixth graders' Web page "book" about U.S. history to Mrs. Newborn's first and second graders' exhibits on the solar system. Miss Harris's fifth-grade class told us all about ancient civilizations from prehistoric times through the Renaissance ("It was like a big bloom in history"), the Middle Ages, Rome, Greece, and Egypt. *The Mad Scientist*, developed for grades 4–6, takes you through the scientific method, provides classroom experiments (there's a new one each week, with at least one question your students answer via e-mail), special topics, a teacher's guide, and a glossary. Mrs. Sava's first graders shared their games, paintings, dioramas, poems, and even a puppet show they created for their rain forest unit, and Mr. Smith's fifth graders shared their tessellations. Be sure to check Mrs. Coakley's sixth-grade page because each week a new problem is presented. You are invited to e-mail your own solutions and compare them with those submitted by her students. We're still busy working on one of them right now ("How many guests were present at a Chinese dinner if every two guests shared a bowl of rice, every three guests shared a bowl of broth, and every four guests shared a bowl of meat and 65 bowls were used all together?"). You will also want to continue to watch the progress of sixth-grade students taking the elective class "Designing Web Pages," as they create a virtual interactive tour of their school. Other students will take you on a tour of their hometown and the Commonwealth of Virginia.

UNITED STATES—WASHINGTON

Glenwood Heights Primary School

See Chapter 1—U.S. History—Lewis and Clark Expedition.

UNITED STATES—WASHINGTON, D.C.

Lincoln Memorial

http://www.nps.gov/linc/index2.htm

Take a tour of the Lincoln Memorial with the U.S. National Park Service. You will be able to travel back in time during the decade it took to build the memorial. Learn about the collaborations between sculptor Daniel Chester French, architect Henry Bacon, and muralist Jules Guerin. The tour includes lessons on architecture, President Abraham Lincoln, and the social climate of the times. Your students may be interested to learn that at the dedication of the memorial (1922), the keynote speaker, Dr. Robert Martin, president of the Tuskegee Institute, was not allowed to sit at the speakers' platform and had to find seating in the section of the lawn reserved for African Americans.

National Cathedral

See Chapter 2—Architecture Through the Ages.

UNITED STATES—WISCONSIN

Northwoods

http://northernwisconsin.com

The Northern Wisconsin Tourism, Travel, and Outdoor Information Network has developed *Kids Pages* to keep your students busy throughout the year with crafts and science projects. They probably won't realize they are learning as they make wild rice popcorn and snow ice cream. While reading the recipe for snow ice cream, for example, they will learn that the Inuit people have more than 50 words for snow, including *ganik* (snow that is still falling), *pukaq* (crust snow), and *masak* (mushy snow). Officials will also show you how to identify trees without their leaves and introduce you to the local loon population. Dr. Loonacy is looking forward to sharing his extensive knowledge about loons with you. Did you know that the birds are so large that they need about a quarter mile of lake surface to build up enough speed to fly? It's not surprising when you learn that some of the loons have been clocked at 80 miles per hour. The site also has some hidden geography lessons as students tour the northern part of the state through interactive maps.

UNITED STATES—WYOMING

Sunflower Elementary School

http://cyberkids.ccsd.k12.wy.us/sunflower/tittle.html

Learn all about Wyoming from the K–6 students at Sunflower Elementary School in Gillette. Mrs. Todd's fourth-grade class would love to share their research on cowboys, mountain men, and the Oregon Trail. Their teacher says, "Parts may not be completely historically accurate or politically correct, but this is how we remember our lesson." She asks that you send e-mail and let her and the class know what you think. Mrs. Geis's fourth graders will share stories about their trips to the local fish hatchery and Fort Phil Kearney, and Mrs. Carney's class will tell you about their trip to Jacobs Ranch Coal mine, which produces more than 4,000 tons of coal per hour. They will show you some of the heavy equipment like the Dressor 830 E truck that hauls 240 tons of coal at a time (you have to be very careful because each tire costs $12,000). The fifth graders went to the Wyodak Mine, where they learned how coal is used to create steam to make electricity. Other classes have been busy making friends in Detroit and learning about whales and Australia. Mrs. Geis's class is also participating in the "travel buddies" program and has sent the McMoosey Brothers to do their traveling for them.

For more information about the travel buddies program, see Chapter 3— Travel Buddies.

WORLDWIDE TRAVEL

See also Chapter 3—Travel Buddies.

Tour 1

http://www.ipl.org/youth

Students can tour the world with Parsifal Penguin and Olivia Owl, courtesy of the Internet Public Library Youth Services Division. Parsifal and Olivia's worldwide tour will enable students to learn about holidays and festivals, sample international cuisine, play games such as the Kenyan game jackstones, visit local museums, and read folktales. Parsifal tells us that he is ready to learn about culture—he has spent his entire life in Antarctica, where "there is no culture to speak of—just a few research stations where people eat freeze dried spam and play checkers." Countries change periodically. On our last visit we went to Brazil, where we learned about *Gato Doente* (Sick Cat), a game of tag in which the players who are "Ait" have to hold the part of their body that's been tagged.

Tour 2—National Geographic

http://www.nationalgeographic.com/main.html

The National Geographic Society has 600 tours available, each with a map that can be downloaded. Just click anywhere on the worldwide map, and you are off. In case you want to tour the world of the future, take your class to the Millennium exhibit, which has maps of the future; presentations on ecological, social, and political projections; and a forum where people around the globe post their e-mail responses to questions such as, "Where have all the flowers gone?" The forum is unmoderated, and many of the postings are from adults, so you may want to screen this part first.

Tour 3—United Nations

http://www.un.org/Pubs/CyberSchoolBus

There is something of interest for all students in grades K–12 on this tour sponsored by the United Nations (UN). Tours, conducted in English, Spanish, and French, cover a variety of global issues, and there's always a UN ambassador available to chat with your students. Be sure to stop by the *Quiz Quad,* where guides teach world facts, geography, health, and environmental issues through quizzes and games. Meet the professor, who travels around the world and sends postcards about her experiences—of course, you will have to figure out what country she's writing from. For example, the postcard from Australia says, "Thanks to Laeng, here are: 300,000 pitoti in Permian sandstone carved by the Camunni and polished by the wurm glacier." The *Resource Source* includes an extensive database containing profiles of 185 countries and cities. Be sure to stop by *The Gallery* to view the photographs by UN staff photographer John Isaac. Teachers will want to check the latest projects at the *Curriculum Corner,* where students are able to join in activities with classes throughout the world covering such issues as land mines and human rights. Younger students will enjoy the *Elementary Planet,* where they can play a game of *Flag Tag*, color, or play *The Urban Fact Game.*

Tour 4

http://www.greatestplaces.org

Travel to some of the most geographically dynamic locations on earth, courtesy of the National Science Foundation and the Science Museum of Minnesota. Last time we checked, tours were available to the Amazon, Greenland, Iguaçú Falls, Madagascar, Namibia, and Tibet. Each spot you choose to visit covers current issues, culture, and lots of interesting facts. On the Amazon tour, for example, we learned that the sound often heard in jungle movies can't be heard in a real jungle—it's actually a laughing Australian kookaburra. Be sure not to miss Madagascar, where students can learn about lemurs, watch a chameleon, listen to a giant hissing bug, and find out why the baobab is the national symbol. There's a lot of activities to keep your students busy, including recipes and experiments. They can find out, for example, what melting ice cubes have to do with glaciers, ocean currents, and Greenland. You can also add your favorite place to the list of tours. Just fill out the forms on-site, which help your students describe what there is to do, why you think its great, how to get there, and its precise location. Help is available for figuring out the longitude and latitude of a place or using global positioning systems (satellite technology).

CHAPTER 4

DOWN ON THE FARM

Why are state and county fairs always held during the summertime when school is not in session? Now you can bring your class to fairs any time during the year or visit hog, chicken, soybean, corn, and even alpaca farms, where you can learn the latest innovations in agriculture from universities and down-home farmers. Whether you want information on eggs, asparagus, pork, beans, miniature donkeys, or goats, we've found applicable tours.

4-H KIDS INFORMATIONAL DIRT ROAD
http://www.ics.uci.edu/~pazzani/4H/InfoDirtRoad.html

Local children have been very busy working at the 4-H cooperative farm at the University of California at Irvine. They are quite proud of their efforts and would like you to get to know their goats, sheep, and swine. There are pictures, sounds, movies, and narratives in which they share their daily activities. They will tell you all about how to raise and care for animals, some of the common diseases, and how to get animals ready for showing. You will see more female than male animals—the children tell us that they are easier to manage and have less offensive odors.

AGRICULTURAL SCAVENGER HUNT
http://www.agriquest.com

Take your students on an agricultural Internet scavenger hunt, courtesy of the Canadian Animal Health Institute. Students are provided with multiple choice questions about farm animals and products and links to Internet sites where the answers may be found. It's a good way to introduce students to basic Internet research and hypertext links.

ALPACAS

http://www.alpacanet.com

This site contains alpaca facts (the average alpaca can yield enough fiber to make four to six sweaters per shearing), history, and health information. You can even find out where to buy one.

BARNYARD BUDDIES

http://www.execpc.com/~byb/indexa.html

Children can visit with all of their *Barnyard Buddy* friends: Mike the Mule, Gary the Goat, Polly the Pig, Sofie the Sheep, Bruce the Bull, Roberta the Rabbit, and Randy the Rooster will tell you about the food they eat and how it isn't really that much different from what you eat (or what you should be eating, if you want to be healthy). You can also play trivia and board games with your buddies or spend some time coloring posters of your friends. You will love the online copy of *Circus Champions,* with scenes and stories from the video. This site is loaded with commercials, so stay within the sections we've described.

CORN WORLD

http://www.point-and-click.com/corn

Did you know that 1 bushel of corn will yield enough sweetener for more than 400 cans of soda? The Ohio Corn Marketing Project will tell your students everything about corn and corn products. This crop, produced on every continent with the exception of Antarctica, is used in more than 3,500 products, including packing peanuts and baby diapers. A special *Kid's Corner* has dozens of interesting experiments and projects. Students can find out, for example, if the amount of water in a kernel will affect its popping ability, how to make biodegradable plastic, and how seeds grow in different soils. There is also a special section on the production of ethanol.

COUNTY FAIR

http://www.mda.state.mi.us/kids/index.html

Pay a visit to a county fair in Michigan, courtesy of the state's Department of Agriculture. Students may choose to visit the animal or crop exhibits or learn about food safety from Booster Rooster. The animal exhibit covers sheep, pigs, lambs, turkeys, bunnies, and chicks and includes a history of each animal, pictures, facts, movies, and sounds. Ten-year-old Megan will tell you why the next time someone tells you that you eat like a pig, you should say "thank you." The crop section covers cherries, soybeans, asparagus, sugar, and Easter lilies. You will learn that soybeans are used in over 140 products and that asparagus originated in ancient Greece and Rome. If you have time, you can also learn how maple syrup and apple cider are made and pay a visit to some local farm families.

FAMILY FARM PROJECT
http://www.kenyon.edu/projects/famfarm

Kenyon College's Family Farm Project explores family and community life in Knox County, Ohio. The organization and materials of this site make it ideal for upper grade classes in environmental studies, social studies, family studies, business, and economics. A family farm is defined not by size but rather by the unconditional involvement of family members in the enterprise. Your students will be able to learn about technology, myths and stereotypes, dangers, and typical daily chores and understand how and why farmers use economics, veterinary medicine, mechanics, land-use planning, business, biology, government regulations, and computers in their everyday life. There is also a section on the Amish and how the organization and operation of their family farms differ from those that use electricity and machinery.

FARMER'S ALMANAC
http://www.almanac.com

The *Farmer's Almanac* was first published in 1792 when George Washington was president. Since that time it has published useful information, including tide tables, sunrise tables, planting charts, recipes, and weather predictions. This site presents a history of the almanac as well as typical information presented in the complete publication. Students can check the five-day and long-range weather forecasts and see how accurate they really are. In 1792 publishers claimed they had a secret formula that enabled them to make predictions with 80 percent accuracy, and you may want to have your class check it for accuracy. Check out *Heavenly Details* for dates and locations of solar and lunar eclipses as well as the dates of the full moon for the next seven years. You can also look up the rising and setting of the sun, moon, and planets for any location in the United States. Administrators publish daily historical events, advice of the day, and weekly wisdom ("It's of no use to carry an umbrella if your shoes are leaky.")

FOWL
http://www.cyborganic.com/People/feathersite/index.html

From the Hudson River Valley in New York, Barry Koffler, former ecology major and current writer/editor/proofreader/computer whiz, invites your students to learn all about chickens, ducks, geese, guinea fowl, pea fowl, swans, and turkeys. The *Poultry Glossary* includes photographs, videos, and information about hundreds of species of fowl, presented in a lively and easily understandable style. For instance, we were told, "All chickens are chickens. They all hatch out as chicks. Young males are cockerels and become roosters at one year of age. Young females are pullets and become hens at one year."

GOATS
http://home.earthlink.net/~lureynolds/index.html

Luke Walker Reynolds of Indiana University wants you to know that there are more people in the world who consume products from goats than from cows. This site, suggested for high school students, presents information and photographs covering the various breeds of goats, which include the Nubian, pygmy, Boer (bred for meat), and cashmere and angora, which are bred for fur. Students will learn how goats help the environment, the products they provide, and how to care for them.

ILLINOIS DEPARTMENT OF AGRICULTURE
http://www.state.il.us/agr/kidspage

The goal of this Illinois Department of Agriculture site is to let visitors know that agriculture is more than farming. A visit to this site covers the broad scope of agriculture, including turning crops and livestock into consumable products, transportation, caring for sick animals, producing equipment, and protecting the environment. Geared toward lower-level grades, materials include tours of farms, quizzes that allow students to test their "agriculture IQs," and word searches and games. Students will learn, for example, that corn is used in more than 4,000 products, including soda pop, chewing gum, potato chips, jelly, catsup, and even fireworks.

THE INCREDIBLE EDIBLE EGG
http://www.aeb.org

The American Egg Board hosts this site to provide information to egg consumers, producers, and processors. Students can learn how egg cartons are dated and graded, the parts of an egg, labeling laws, and nutritional facts. You can even learn what to do if you drop an egg on the floor (sprinkle it heavily with salt, and you should have no problems with cleanup). Be sure to check the *Eggcyclopedia*, a glossary that covers everything you want to know about the egg, including the origin of the terms *egghead* and *egg money*. It even has an accurate explanation of cholesterol.

LIVESTOCK
http://www.ansi.okstate.edu/breeds

The Department of Animal Science at Oklahoma State University has provided information on anything you might want to know about various breeds of livestock from Texas longhorns to Tibetan yaks. Each breed listing includes illustrations, descriptions, and history and origin. They can also argue that raising livestock is an efficient use of land.

MINIATURE DONKEYS
http://www.qis.net/~minidonk/donktext.htm

What stands only 36 to 38 inches high, lives to be 25 to 40 years old, and requires a lot of personal attention? The male is called a jack and the female is called a jennet, and they are both very loving as long as you are not a dog. We're talking about miniature donkeys. Publishers of *Miniature Donkey Talk Magazine* and personnel from the International Miniature Donkey Registry share their photographs, their knowledge of husbandry, and information on the care, breeding, and history of these lovable creatures. Be sure to check out *Donkey Details,* where you will learn about color, health care, reproduction, feeding, personality traits, methods of communication, costs, and other fascinating information. There are even miniature donkeys for sale—check out the photos and prices.

NATIONAL PORK PRODUCER'S COUNCIL
http://www.nppc.org/foodfun.html

The National Pork Producer's Council will take your students on a tour of an Iowa pig farm, where they will be able to follow the daily life of a pig from conception to appearances at the local 4-H fair. Students will also be able to travel around the world with pork as they take an interactive voyage through a magical pantry. The voyage begins by selecting one of the ethnic foods stored in the pantry. Choosing rice, for example, will take you to China, where you can join a family for *jeng tsan* (dinner) and learn how to eat with chopsticks. Any of the tours, which currently include Hawaii, the Caribbean, and Spain, include recipes, crafts, and information about local culture and people. There is also information about of food safety and nutrition. Teachers will be especially interested in the lesson plans. Additional free educational materials that can also be ordered online.

OHIO HOKSHICHANKIYA FARM COMMUNITY
http://www.users.hockinghills.net/~hokshi/

The Hokshichankiya clan of the Cherokees invites your class to their peaceable farm community in southeastern Ohio, where they can meet the clan members and their animals and learn about Cherokee rituals, holidays and beliefs. In addition to the usual farm residents like chickens, goats, horses, and pigs, your class will also meet a buffalo and Sung Manitu Tanka, a full-blooded wolf who lives on the farm. If you plan to be near the area, check their 3-month calendar of ceremonies and events: the clan, pronounced, Hok-she-chahn-key-yah, invites you to participate, if you're sincere, in everything from their solstice sunrise ceremony to their sweat lodge and sacred pipe rituals. If you're not planning to be near Ohio in the future, you're still more than welcome to e-mail them. Chief Sun Hawk and his wife, Joy Hummingbird, who remind your students to "walk in Peace, with the Wind at your back and the gentle warmth of Father Sun on your face."

SHEEP

American Sheep Industry Association

http://www.sheepusa.org

The American Sheep Industry Association provides information on sheep, lambs, and wool. There are recipes and nutritional information, tips on food safety and storage, and a tour of sheep country. Students will learn how sheep are raised and how to care for the animals. The special kid's section has quizzes, games, projects, and useful information, such as the difference between fine, medium, and coarse wool. Students in grades 4-6 can participate in an Internet scavenger hunt—a research project that uses the Internet to find agriculture-related answers.

Groveland Farm

http://www.impossibledream.com/sheep

Mare and Rusty Jarvis, friendly folks, invite you on a tour of Groveland Farm in Poplar, Wisconsin, along the south shore of Lake Superior. Be sure to dress properly because it gets cold up there, and it's not uncommon for more than 39 inches of snow to accumulate. This is a great climate for raising sheep, however, and Mare and Rusty will share their extensive collection of sheep photographs and tell you all about the various breeds and their history. There is an extensive section on milking sheep. Sheep dairying, a new industry in the United States, has been practiced for years in Europe and the Middle East. Sheep are actually better for the environment than cows because five sheep will eat the same amount of grass as one cow. You can even learn all about sheep farm management and how to do a proper business plan. There's also a section on wool, but be careful with those shears. We found out that after they are sheared, the sheep need some help in learning how to recognize each other once again. Mare and Rusty invite your class to e-mail or call them, but they want you to remember that they are in the Central time zone, and they are not night owls, so telephone during school hours.

TEXAS A&M'S AGROPOLIS

http://agprogram.tamu.edu/agropolis

AGropolis is the place to visit if you want to learn how to grow gardens and crops, take care of your pets and livestock, become more environmentally responsible, and learn about food preparation and safety. This site, sponsored by Texas A&M's University System Agricultural Program, is geared toward upper-level grades, and the diversity of the material makes it impossible for us to summarize. Let's just say you can find out about anything from genetic engineering to recipes to choosing the right pumpkin. The material includes videos, scholarly and popular magazine articles, and tours of the university's various departments. Much of the material is also available in Spanish.

VIRTUAL RANCH TOUR
http://www.kidsfarm.com

Spend some time with the people and animals on this ranch on the western slope of the Colorado Rockies. The music is great! There are horses, cattle, dogs, sheep, goats, ducks, turkeys, geese, chickens, and llamas—each of which has a unique personality. Jack and Jill, Belgian draft horses, spend most of their time together. Jill is rather docile, but Jack is very selfish and jealous. He gets very angry when Jill is being groomed and fed and tries to chase her away by kicking and biting. We didn't want to get involved, so we spent some time with the cattle and learned how to read a brand. If you get tired of the animals, you can spend some time picking cherries or learning about the local wildflowers, apples, and hay. You can also learn how to operate the heavy equipment. Make sure you leave yourself enough time to visit the wildlife and rehabilitation hospital, where they are currently caring for coyotes, bobcats, owls, porcupines, skunks, mountain lions, elk, and deer. Pay attention—sometimes it's hard to concentrate while the cow elk clatter and the bull elk bugle. And you might want to have some tomato juice handy. It's about the only way to get rid of the skunk odor should you happen to get sprayed. The animals at the hospital are not feeling well, and they sometimes get a bit crabby. You will also want to attend the Little Britches Rodeo and watch barrel races, mutton busting, calf roping, and goat tying. Some of the participants are under the age of eight! Check the *Teachers* section for free materials that the rehabilitation center will send to your class. There are calendars and personalized greeting cards signed by one of the ranch animals. Sometimes, they will even let your class name one of the newborns.

WHEAT MANIA
http://www.hpj.com/wsdocs/whearts/whearts.htm

Wacky Wheat spends his days showing visitors around Kansas wheat country. He'll take you to see a Kansas wheat farm and prairie skyscrapers (silos) and even play super trivia and "Flour Power" fun and games. Be sure to visit his friends on their farms, where they will take you through an entire wheat season from planting to harvest. Did you know that in 1990, Kansas farmers produced enough wheat to provide every person in the world with six loaves of bread, and there was still enough left over to produce cat litter, wheat concrete, biodegradable spoons and forks, and other products?

CHAPTER 5

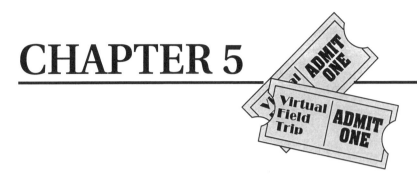

MOTHER NATURE

All the wonders of Mother Nature are available to your class, from the earth's oldest living botanical resident to worldwide botanical gardens. Your students can see alligators, aardvarks, guide dogs, moose, mice, bats, butterflies, and baboons. Check out earthquakes, see what we can do about tigers or what they can do to you, take a dip in the ocean to see some reefs dating back to the Jurassic period, and watch albatrosses crisscross the globe without having to worry about them bringing you any bad luck.

See also Chapter 4—Down on the Farm.

ANCIENT BRISTLECONE PINE
http://www.sonic.net/bristlecone/index.html

The earth's oldest living resident was discovered in 1953 in the White-Inyo mountain range in California. "Methuselah," a 4,764-year-old bristlecone pine tree, was a seedling while the pyramids were being constructed. In addition to providing several beautiful photos for downloading, Leonard Miller, a California glass artist, tells about this species of tree in the language of poetic science. Learn how even dead bristlecone pines survive for centuries as a result of their high resinous content, which repels bacteria that decompose other trees. Miller's story about how a student, with the permission of the U.S. Forest Service, cut down and killed the oldest living thing on Earth will have your own students think twice about carving their initials in trees.

THE ANIMAL KINGDOM

See also Chapter 3—Amazonia *and* Chapter 4—Down on the Farm.

American Alligator

http://gnv.ifas.ufl.edu/www/agator/htm/aligator.htm

The official reptile of the state of Florida will eat almost anything. If you don't believe us, check the photographs of the stomach contents of an alligator at this University of Florida Institute of Food and Agricultural Sciences site. Administrators will tell you all about alligators, including where they live, what they eat, how big they get, and what to do if you encounter one. Note: When typing this web address, be sure to spell "alligator" with one "l."

Animals of the Arctic

http://tqjunior.advanced.org/3500/index.htm

Students can sit in a warm classroom while traveling across one of the coldest places on Earth. Administrators of this site will introduce them to the animals that thrive in the eight nations whose territory crosses the Arctic Circle—from the Arctic fox to the walrus. For a firsthand experience of what some of the animals endure to survive, check the activities and learn how to make blubber mittens. It takes a lot of energy to thrive in this climate. In fact, most bugs crawl rather than fly in order to conserve energy. The Arctic tern is one of the exceptions. This tiny bird (only 12–15 inches long and weighing less than 2 pounds) migrates more than 22,000 miles and almost never lands. Mr. and Mrs. Herman, Cup'ik Alaskans, will share some of their stories about life in the Arctic and how they keep busy. Students can learn how to do scrimshaw using ivory soap, make animal carvings, and study owl pellets. If you want a memento of your trip, send away for some of the free posters offered on-site.

Bat Conservation International

http://www.batcon.org

Bat Conservation International would like you to know that bats are not blind, they are not rodents, and they will not get caught in your hair. In addition to dispelling popular myths, the organization provides bat descriptions and pictures, facts and trivia, and even recordings of bat's echolocation calls. You will want to check the educator's activity book. Although they are offering this publication for sale, they have provided free puzzles, games, and activities.

Bats for Younger Students

http://members.aol.com/bats4kids

Merlin Tuttle, a bat enthusiast, has designed this site especially for kids to help them learn to like, respect, and help protect bats. Through simple texts, games, and quizzes, he'll tell you where bats live, what they eat, and what they look like. Mr. Tuttle will even take you on a visit to a bat cave and tell teachers how they may invite a bat into their classroom.

Dogs—Guide Dogs

http://penny.myriad.net

Penny, a golden retriever puppy training to be a guide dog for the visually impaired, wants to meet your students and share her photographs and stories with them. She has been hanging around schools most of her life. Penny was born at the Bryker Woods Elementary School in Austin, where her mom was part of a unit on mammals. She then went to live at the Sam Rayburn Middle School in Bryan, Texas, with her "puppy walker," art teacher Becker Alter. The students raised money to buy the puppy by collecting pennies. Penny will tell you how puppies are selected for the guide dog program and how they are trained. She'll even introduce you to some of her friends from the canine world and to her special friend Daniel, a boy with autism.

Dogs—Ralston Purina's World of Dogs

http://www.purina.com/dogs/index.html

Ralston Purina will tell your students everything about dogs, including nutrition, training and behavior, grooming, and operating a kennel. Students can find the breed best suited to their individual temperaments and lifestyles by taking the interactive survey that asks them to choose such traits as size, energy level, temperament, coat, and so on. Or, they can choose dogs that have been matched to existing profiles, such as apartment dwellers or working moms. Some students might even discover that they are not suited for owning a dog.

Endangered Species—American Museum of Natural History

http://www.amnh.org/Exhibition/Expedition/Endangered/index.html

Students can spend hours wandering through the halls of the American Museum of Natural History's *EnDANGERed Exhibition,* where they can view some of the last remaining Siberian tigers, radiated tortoises, Chinese alligators, and other animals and habitats. Be sure to watch the *Legend of the Meeps Island Flying Frog* and see how this creature was brought to the brink of extinction and back. They will also learn how the introduction of the Nile perch almost caused the doom of Lake Victoria and the human population that depends on the lake by destroying the ecological balance. Or they can see before-and-after photographs of a Volkswagen Beetle that, a few years after it sank in a lake, was covered with zebra mussels.

Endangered Species—U.S. Fish and Wildlife Service

http://www.fws.gov/r9edspp.html

The U.S. Fish and Wildlife Service presents photographs and information about endangered species. Materials are classified by geographic location as well as categorically by vertebrate and invertebrate animals and flowering and nonflowering plants. Be sure to visit the *Kids Corner,* which will tell you where to find further information, what you and your school can do to help (they tell us that "endangered means there's still time"), and where teachers can get free educational materials. There are also games and puzzles offering interesting challenges. Find out "whether you are a sagacious scientist or a laser-witted layperson. Barrage your brain with a batter of beastly biology questions bound to bolster your blossoming knowledge."

Moose

See Chapter 3—United States—Alaska—Anne Hopkins Wein Elementary School.

Tigers

http://www.5tigers.org

The Tiger Information Center, a program sponsored by the National Fish and Wildlife Foundation and hosted by the Minnesota Zoo, is dedicated to providing information that will help preserve the remaining five subspecies of tigers—the Siberian, South China, Indochinese, Bengal, and Sumatran tigers. Materials include an interactive tiger reference book with animation, pictures and sounds, and projects and reports submitted by worldwide experts. There is a special section devoted to younger students and their teachers that has a wealth of information, facts, and pictures (we loved the *Tiger Guts* photograph) organized by grade level. Students will learn why tigers have stripes, how fast they can travel, and whether or not they really eat people. There are a series of interactive simulation games that appeal to all ages. The games provide valuable information about poaching, regulations, and preservation.

ARBORETUMS AND BOTANIC GARDENS

Brooklyn Botanic Garden

http://www.bbg.org

Most people do not realize that the New York metropolitan area includes beaches, dunes, pine barrens, oak forests, lakes, streams, swamps, bogs, and cliffs that serve as habitat for more than 2,750 species of plants. Scientists at the Brooklyn Botanic Garden have provided a comprehensive guide to local woody plants. They will help you identify plants through a series of onscreen prompts. There are also direct links to encyclopedias and glossaries where students can further research their finds. Keep checking this site because there are plans to expand the information to cover many other types of local flora.

Devonian Botanic Garden

http://www.discoveredmonton.com/devonian/dbg.html

Tours of the University of Alberta's Devonian Botanic Garden take you through the alpine, herb, butterfly, and native people's gardens. The latter is of specific note because extensive research has been conducted about the medicinal properties of hundreds of plants. Botanists will share their knowledge about such plants as *Geum triflorum,* or "Old Man's Whiskers," used by the Blackfoot tribe as a perfume; an eyewash; a treatment for sore gums and saddle sores, chicken pox, snow blindness, and chapped lips; and a food to help horses gain weight.

Japanese Garden at California State University

http://www.csulb.edu/~jgarden

Computer engineering students from California State University at Long Beach not only want to take your class on a tour of their serene and dramatic Japanese Garden, but they also want to replicate the sense of contemplation and tranquillity for them. Loraine Miller Collins (who funded the garden) stated at the garden's dedication in 1981: "When a person is tired, or anxious, or in quest of beauty, may they enter and come forth refreshed to meet the problems of the day. . . . There will be serenity as you walk around the lake, and joy, I hope in the beauty of the reflections in that lake. And, of course, there will be bamboo. . . . There is an old proverb that says, 'Bamboo bends but never breaks.' It is my hope that as you leave your tour of the garden, you will find in your heart that proverb, and the day will be filled with joy." The tour downplays technical information during its 16 stops at places such as the Moon Bridge or the Votive Stone. As your class pauses at the Rankei Lantern, for example, they are reminded of the five cardinal virtues of Zen: humanity, justice, politeness, wisdom, and fidelity.

Memorial University of Newfoundland's Botanic Garden

http://www.mun.ca/botgarden

While managing to grow 2.5-pound onions, botanists at Memorial University still find the time to take you on guided tours of their facilities. Feel free to wander as long as you like through the cottage, wildlife, heritage, dried flower, and rock gardens, the rhododendron dell, or the ericaceous border. The botanists are more than willing to share their research and gardening tips and will even let you hear their collection of bird calls.

Missouri Botanical Gardens

http://www.mobot.org/welcome.html

There are more than 79 acres and 30 gardens at this extensive site. Of particular interest is the Japanese garden, where tours are offered in either English or French. This is a *chisen kaiyu-shiki* (wet strolling garden), a style developed by wealthy landowners of the late Edo period in nineteenth-century Japan. Kioichi Kawana, a designer of the garden, said: "A Japanese garden cannot be fully explained in words, but must be experienced. The garden must be seen with the mind, not just the eye, to grasp the deeper spiritual meaning." Students will be able to have this experience while learning such gardening concepts as *meigakkure* (the quality of remaining hidden from ordinary view). Be sure to check the *Feature of the Month*. When we last checked, *Kohler's Medizinal Pflanzen*, a reproduction of the original three-volume set of illustrations featuring European plants of medicinal interest, was featured. The volumes were published in the 1800s using chromolithography (the process of rendering images on stone or zinc plates and filling them with colored inks). Also, be sure to stop by the *Image Gallery,* which features weekly plants in bloom.

Southwestern Arboretum

http://ag.arizona.edu/BTA

Boyce Thompson's Southwestern Arboretum is the American Southwest's oldest arboretum and botanical garden. Virtual tours include the facility's cactus and legume gardens as well as desert wildflowers and birds. Dr. Frank S. Crosswhite will share his knowledge about growing succulent plants. History buffs may prefer to meet Colonel William Boyer Thompson, the former mining magnate who founded the arboretum.

State Botanical Garden of Georgia

http://www.uga.edu/~botgarden

The University of Georgia has set aside a 313-acre preserve as a living laboratory. Enter through the butterfly's fluttering wings, for a walk through natural areas and trails while viewing the international, rose, native flora, annual and perennial, or dahlia gardens. Of particular interest is the trial garden, where shrubs and trees are planted for the purpose of testing their adaptability to the southeastern U.S. climate.

University of British Columbia's Botanic Gardens

http://www.hedgerows.com/UBCBotGdn

This Vancouver facility overlooking the Strait of Georgia encompasses 70 acres with more than 10,000 types of trees, shrubs, and flowers. The university is a leader in plant introduction research and will share its knowledge with your students. Tours of the various alpine, Asian, winter, and native gardens are available, each of which represents a unique geographic area.

BIG BEND NATIONAL PARK

http://geoweb.tamu.edu/faculty/herbert/bigbend

Take a tour of Big Bend National Park in West Texas, adjacent to the Rio Grande, courtesy of Professor Bruce Herbert and his students from Texas A&M's Department of Geology. The tour includes some of the park's most interesting features, such as the Chisos Mountains, Mule Ear Peaks, Santa Elena Canyon, and Persimmon Gap. Through techniques of geologic interpretation used by scientists, students have reconstructed a geologic timeline that delineates significant periods in the development of Big Bend. The igneous, metamorphic, and sedimentary processes are explained, and photographs of the unique land formations caused by each are shown. The less scientifically oriented might prefer the 4.6-mile round-trip hike along Lost Mine Trail. You will have to be in fairly good shape because the trail begins at an elevation of 5,600 feet and ascends to 6,850 feet in just 2.3 miles. Trail markers along the way point out some of the most interesting sites, such as the Mexican pinyon pine tree, which thrives at elevations above 4,800 feet, and the alligator juniper, named after its textured bark.

BIRD-WATCHING

The Albatross Project

http://www.wfu.edu/albatross

Students from all over the world are joining with scientists to track albatrosses in Hawaii using space satellites, navigational transmitters, and e-mail. Your class is invited to join the project—a joint venture of North Carolina's Wake Forest University and the U.S. National Science Foundation. Scientists are trying to find out where the birds go when they leave their nesting islands, how they move, what they do, and what they like and dislike. They've already found out many interesting things that they will share during this tour. For example, the birds are excellent athletes, lay only one egg (the size of a can of Coca-Cola), and practice some unusual child-care techniques. Your students can see how they compare in size to an albatross—Kate, a fifth grader, has a "wingspan" of 1.4 meters, Michael Jordan can span 2.1 meters, and an albatross spans 3.5 meters—4½ feet, 7 feet, and 11 ½ feet, respectively. The tour also shows your students how satellites work, how to analyze tracking data, and how to use a flight distance calculator.

Hummingbirds

http://www.derived.net/hummers

If you want a close-up view of a hummingbird, wear red clothing. Hummingbirds find their food visually (they have no sense of smell) and will swoop down to see if you are a food source. Administrators of this site have compiled a wealth of information, facts, and advice about the birds, feeders, gardens, nectar formulas, and natural history. You can learn how to attract, watch, and study all 17 North American hummingbird species. Migration status maps are provided, so you will know the most opportune time to conduct your observations. You may also participate in the annual hummingbird mapping project—a new species is mapped each year.

Loons

See Chapter 3—United States—Wisconsin—Northwoods.

BUREAU OF LAND MANAGEMENT

http://www.blm.gov/education/education.html

The U.S. Bureau of Land Management (BLM) would like to share its 270-million-acre nationwide laboratory with your students. Tours cover a variety of topics, including the life cycle of salmon, wildflower exploration, migratory patterns of neotropical birds, and the study and discovery of plants and animals. Pay a visit to the Sonoran Desert ecosystem and participate in activities that simulate land-planning decisions and explore the adaptations made by local flora and fauna to survive in the desert. Or stop by the Columbia River basin and experience the challenges faced by natural resource managers while learning scientific concepts behind hydroelectric power, and socio-scientific issues such as the conflict between protecting historic salmon runs and providing inexpensive electricity through hydropower. Join the BLM explorers as they investigate caves and other natural phenomena, or learn about riparian areas or the role of fire and noxious weeds in the maintenance of ecosystems.

BUTTERFLY WATCHING

Essig Museum of Entomology at Berkeley

http://www.mip.berkeley.edu/essig

This Berkeley institution, which was established in 1940, houses one of the largest and most active collections of arthropods in the United States. Approximately 4.5 million specimens are maintained. Administrators of the site concentrate on endangered California species such as the Lotis Blue butterfly. There are many pictures as well as descriptions, reasons for extinction, and information about current conservation efforts. Your students will also be able to take a tour of threatened California habitats such as vernal pools, coastal dunes, riparian woodlands, and desert springs.

U.S. Geological Survey Site

http://www.mesc.usgs.gov/butterfly/Butterfly.html

The Children's Butterfly Website, sponsored by the U.S. Geological Survey, is run by Paul Opler, a retired employee. Opler can tell your students where to find the country's 12,000–15,000 species of butterflies and 150,000–250,000 species of moths, describe how to catch them, and even explain how they "go to the bathroom." There are coloring pages showing the life cycle of the monarch butterfly, beautiful photographs, links to sites with other pictures, and distribution maps of butterflies and moths in North America. Your class can also e-mail butterfly questions and read the questions (and answers) from other students.

EARTHQUAKES

http://www.crustal.ucsb.edu/ics/understanding

Travel to this site and get ready to shake, rattle, and roll. The University of California at Santa Barbara will take your students on a scientific, historical, and visceral tour of earthquakes and fault lines, complete with animation, photographs, and a rotating globe showing earthquake locations. Mark Twain, Jack London, Charles Darwin, and John Muir share their eyewitness accounts of earthquakes.

GLACIER NATIONAL PARK

http://www.sd5.mt.us/glaciereft

Hop on board the red jammer bus for a virtual tour of Glacier National Park. Students will gain an understanding of the ecosystems, botany, geology, glaciers, weather, aquatics, and wildlife comprising the "crown jewel of the Rockies." The team of educators and park officials sponsoring the trip will eventually provide a series of lesson plans and activities covering science, social studies, language arts, and math. Park officials will be available for live "chats" via the Internet.

JURASSIC REEF PARK

http://www.uni-stuttgart.de/UNIuser/igps/edu/JRP

Professor Reinhold Leinfelder, a geologist and paleontologist from the University of Stuttgart, will take you on a trip through reefs dating from the Jurassic period. In a mock commercial tour, Leinfelder uses imaginary tourist brochures and classified ads to introduce the various reefs, but his information is serious and detailed. Students will learn how reefs, one of the most complex ecosystems of our planet, are formed and how they affect the global climate. There's plenty of interesting photographs of coral reefs and their denizens, such as crabs and sponges, and Leinfelder carefully explains the parts each of these organisms plays in the maintenance of the reef ecosystem.

New York State Geology Field Trip

http://www.hartwick.edu/geology/work/VFT-so-far/VFT.html

Retrace the road trip of students from Hartwick College who kept an "electronic road log" across the state of New York from Oneonta to the Hudson River through 400 million years of geologic history. They will tell you how plate tectonics control the distribution and frequency of phenomena such as earthquakes and volcanoes and the distribution of rocks, minerals, natural resources, and living organisms. Stops include the Davenport quarry, with sand, gravel, and cobble deposited by glaciers 14,000 years ago; the Schoharie reservoir, with its sedimentary rocks from the Devonian age; and the tilted strata. After each stop, all of which include explanations of various geological phenomena, you can answer questions to test your knowledge and understanding of what you have learned.

OCEAN

Safari 94—The Barkley Sound Expedition

http://oberon.educ.sfu.ca/splash.htm

In 1994, a team of scientists, divers, archaeologists, and students went on a six-day excursion to explore the ocean environment of Barkley Sound, British Columbia. At the time, the trip was broadcast live into North American and Japanese homes and schools via satellite, and viewers were able to speak directly to the explorers or submit questions via e-mail, fax, or telephone. These communications about marine animal and plant life, shipwrecks, and diving are archived on site. You will able to learn all about sea cucumbers, the largest known octopus (32 feet from arm tip to arm tip and weighing in at 300 pounds), and the fish with the longest life span—the rougheye rockfish, which lives up to 150 years). There are also three-dimensional images, animation, and movies. The site was created by the Exemplary Center for Interactive Technologies in Education (ExCITE) at Simon Fraser University in British Columbia.

PHENOLOGY

http://www.student.wau.nl/~arnold/gpmn.html

Phenology is the study of the recurrence of plant and animal phenomena caused by seasonal changes. This is an interactive site, administered by the Phenology Study Group of the Internet Society of Biometeorology. One of the group's goals is to promote phenology to educators and to teach students about ecological relationships while increasing their observational skills. Check the path *Education/Plantwatch*, which allows students around the world to participate in reporting and mapping the "green wave" of spring all over the globe. They will find there's a lot more to watching plants than they realized!

PINEO RIDGE MORAINE—EASTERN MAINE
http://www.colby.edu/geology/Intro.html

Geology students interested in studying glacial phenomena should not miss this field trip to the Pineo Ridge Moraine/Delta complex in eastern Maine. This area was created about 12,500 years ago, when ice advanced directly into the margins of the Atlantic Ocean. You will see such areas as "the Blueberry Basins," which produce about 95 percent of the U.S. crop, as well as moraines, kettles, flatlands, and forest beds. The trip also includes the Hartford Basin in Connecticut, which developed during the late Triassic and early Jurassic periods.

SMOKEY THE BEAR
http://www.smokeybear.com

The U.S. Forest Service and Smokey the Bear teach fire prevention through games geared toward younger students. Smokey has been too busy dealing with forest fires to have much time to play, so he is asking students to become his e-mail pen pals.

VIRTUAL CAVE
http://www.goodearth.com/virtcave.html

This is one of the best caves you will ever have an opportunity to visit because it includes features from caves around the world. In addition to the usual stalagmites and stalactites, students will be able to see segamites, which occur in only six caves located on the Nullarbor Plain in western Australia, or "bathtubs," which are known to occur only in the Snail Shell Cave in the Gunung Mulu region of Borneo. And don't forget to check out the popcorn, pearls, death coral, and splattermites.

CHAPTER 6

VISUAL ARTS

Take your students from the Enlightenment in France through old New Orleans and into the world of computer-generated design. These virtual field trips include galleries, animated films, art lessons, fashion, design, and photography. We even take you to a place more chaotic than your school lunchroom—inside a van Gogh painting!

ANIMATION

http://wbanimation.warnerbros.com/cmp/ani_04if.htm

How does an idea inside a writer's head eventually become a cartoon? Warner Brothers Studios will take your students through this painstaking process. Students may either choose a specific topic of interest or follow the step-by-step process that covers layout, background, voice and animation artists, music, and the Foley artist who is responsible for sound effects. Along the way, they can watch some videos and read some interviews with people who create the cartoons. Did you know that animators have mirrors by their desks so they can study their own facial expressions?

ART APPRECIATION

A. Pintura—Art Detective

http://www.eduweb.com/pintura

The Case of Grandpa's Painting begins when a woman walks into private detective A. Pintura's office. (You can see through his window into the street while a neon light flashes.) As your students sleuth along with Pintura, they will learn about art history, subject, composition, style, and famous painters. For example, Pintura displays a photograph of Grandpa's painting next to one by Paul Gauguin, and your students decide whether or not the paintings are similar. Their decision determines what happens next in the case. Detective Pintura also provides an art vocabulary list, as well as teacher resources with classroom activities and topics for discussion. Students who don't have a taste for 1940s detective noir stories can play *Inside Art* instead. Be warned—if they choose this option, they will become trapped inside a van Gogh painting and have to answer questions about the painting in order to escape. In the process, they wind up studying the painting in intricate detail and learning about Impressionism and the elements of fine art.

 ## *ART LESSONS*

Art Studio Chalkboard
http://www.saumag.edu/art/studio/chalkboard/paint.html

Ralph Larmann, a fine arts faculty member at Southern Arkansas University, invites you and your students to his studio for free art lessons focusing on the technical fundamentals of showing perspective, shading, using color, painting, and stretching canvases. Textual and visual explanations include pictures of famous works of art that illustrate how fundamental techniques and basics are applied by professional artists and masters. The material is straightforward and precise—ideal for middle- and upper-level students who really want to learn about the technical aspects of painting.

Cartooning
http://www.cartooncorner.com

Emmett Scott will share his extensive knowledge about the art of cartooning with your students. Pay a visit to his *Cartoon Corner* and find out what a cartoonist does and how he does it. Scott even offers free online cartoon lessons. We learned that the most important feature of a cartoon character is the emotion expressed through the eyes, eyebrows, eyelids, and mouth. Scott will also tell you a bit about the four things a cartoonist does—spot drawings, caricatures, editorial cartoons, and animation. For the less artistic, there are puzzles, stories, and riddles.

Electronic Pencil Playground
http://www.drawwithmark.com

Travel to the "farthest reaches of the mind's eye" with illustrator Mark Kistler, who will teach your students to draw figures such as "Speedy Spinach." He'll also share the 12 secrets of three-dimensional drawing. Perhaps your student's work will be chosen for entry into Kistler's on-site *Genius Gallery*.

ART MUSEUMS

See also Chapter 1—French History—Chateau de Versailles.

France's Age of Enlightenment

http://mistral.culture.fr/files/imaginary_exhibition.html

The French Ministry of Culture sponsors this exhibit of paintings, which covers the period from the death of Louis XIV in 1715 to the coup d'état of the 18th Brumaire in 1799, when Napoleon I took power. The exhibit is divided into three primary sections: the Regency (1715–1723), the reigns of Louis XV (1723–1774) and Louis XVI (1774–1792), and the French Revolution of 1789.

Frida Kahlo

http://www.cascade.net/kahlo.html

Mexican artist Frida Kahlo (1907–1954) lived a life of pain caused by childhood polio and a severe automobile accident. Kahlo, who lived with the muralist painter Diego Rivera, used her art to overcome her adversity. Her paintings are powerful, shocking, but also occasionally gentle. In simple language, the site administrator tells Kahlo's story and presents her paintings honestly and factually, without an inspirational veneer. The content may be inspirational for some students and too powerful for others.

Louisiana State Museum

http://www.crt.state.la.us/crt/museum/lsmnet3.htm

The paintings in the Louisiana State Museum focus on the major artistic trends and movements that shaped the state's culture from 1790 to 1950. Paintings and accompanying essays are organized by artist or by genre (portraiture, landscapes, marine paintings, and twentieth century painting). The portrait collection contains French neoclassical portraits of the 1830s and reflects the economic prosperity of antebellum Louisiana from the 1790s to the 1850s. The effects of the state's post–Civil War economic decline and the advent of photography can be traced in the evolution of the collection's landscapes. The museum also has an extensive collection of marine and ship portraits. Of particular note are the works of Captain William Challoner, an amateur artist who painted the ports he frequented as a captain for the Morgan Line, and August Norieri, whose works captured the fading era of steamboats.

For other information contained in this site, see Chapter 1—U.S. History—Louisiana State Museum *and* Chapter 2—New Orleans Historic Buildings.

Metropolitan Museum of Art

http://www.metmuseum.org/htmlfile/opening/enter.html

New York City's Metropolitan Museum of Art has more than two million works of art spanning more than 5,000 years of world culture. The institution's site provides an overview of the collection. Of special interest is the section entitled *Education,* which offers a variety of multimedia experiences. The goal of the museum is to change and expand this site as administrators learn how it is being used by the public. At the current time, an exhibit called *Looking at Art* is featured—an interactive exhibit illustrating the concepts of composition, perspective, light, colors, form, themes, and symbols. There is also a special section for children that at the time of publication showed how art is used to communicate the beliefs and values of the Yoruban people. Children are also encouraged to submit questions by e-mail. Feel free to peruse the archive of frequently asked questions, such as "What's the largest painting in the museum?" or "Who is William?"

Moran, Thomas

See Chapter 12—Moran, Thomas.

National Gallery of Canada

http://national.gallery.ca

Tours of Canada's National Gallery, which are organized around visual and historical themes such as European immigration, are available in either English or French. Curators will share the thoughts of such Canadian artists as David Milne, who said, "Art is not an imitation of anything or a daydream or a memory or vision; it has an existence of its own, an emotion we cannot get from anything in life outside it." Teachers may want to check the section entitled *Resources for Teachers—Slidekits.* In addition to classroom activities such as collages, dances, pantomimes, and observational exercises that will expand students' understanding and experiences of various artists, each kit includes an onscreen slide show. Current slide shows include *M. C. Escher* and *Canada's Indigenous First People.*

Vincent Van Gogh Information Gallery

http://www.openface.ca/~vangogh

"How rich art is; if one can only remember what one has seen, one is never without food for thought or truly alone," quotes David Brooks, who hopes to make his *Vincent Van Gogh Information Gallery* the most thorough and comprehensive repository of the Dutch master's work in existence. Brooks goes to great lengths to point out that he is not a trained artist, critic, or historian. To date, he has accumulated more than 1,965 pages and 1,975 graphics, with more on the way. Van Gogh's works may be viewed by subject matter or alphabetically by the name of the work. Other resources include biographies and articles written by various experts, recent news clippings such as the death of an elderly woman who actually knew van Gogh, and van Gogh "postage stamps" that can be downloaded.

Women in the Arts

http://www.nmwa.org/index.htm

Let the girls show the boys how it's done. Wilhelmina Cole Holladay, the founder of the National Museum of Women in the Arts, conducts this tour of the institution. Your students can accompany her on an audio-video walk through the halls or view paintings and other works of art on their own while reading detailed biographies. The museum's collection honors female painters and artists in other genres from the Renaissance to modern times.

FASHION AND DESIGN

Beverley Birks Couture Collection

http://www.camrax.com/pages/birks0.htm

The Beverley Birks Couture Collection, one of the world's largest haute couture accumulation of accessories, hats, handbags, boots, and shoes, provides your students the opportunity to learn about twentieth-century fashion. The American section includes works from most of the major designers, such as McCardell, Norell, and Gernreich. Other countries represented include England (featuring examples of tailoring and sportswear as well as designs by Liberty of London, Hartnell, Amies, and the English Boutique Movement of the mid- to late-1960s), France (with representative samples from major designers such as Vionett, Chanel, Patou, Dior, and Balenciala), and Italy (a large amount of the collection is devoted to Fortuny and Gallenga). There is also a partial database of the collection, which has approximately 1,000 entries and is 900 pages long. Patterns from major designers will be added at a later date. There are also examples and explanations of *pochoir*—a type of silk screening using up to 30 stencils for one image. The genre began in early-twentieth-century Paris, when the couturier Paul Poiret commissioned a limited-edition album of his fashions.

Goldstein Museum of Design

http://goldstein.che.umn.edu

The Goldstein Museum of Design, located on the St. Paul campus of the University of Minnesota, focuses on how clothing, textiles, and design interact with everyday life in cultures around the world. Current exhibitions are updated monthly, and past exhibitions are archived on-site. Of particular interest is the presentation of the Indian sari, including its history and cultural significance. The families of draping styles, a system for categorizing followed in India, are presented with discussions of how differences and similarities may offer clues as to the origin and migration of people. Other exhibits have featured the work of Gabrielle "Coco" Chanel, who followed the philosophy that "fashion does not exist unless it goes down to the streets. The fashion that remains in the salon has no more significance than a costume ball." Other exhibits include African American quilt making and Cambodian clothing embroidery. Accompanying texts explain the connections between design and culture.

Greek Costume Through the Ages

http://www.firstnethou.com/annam/costhist.html/index.html

This site has been lovingly compiled by Anna Mavromatis of Texas as a tribute to her homeland. Mavromatis covers Greek costuming through the ages, beginning with the Minoan Civilization of 1750–1580 B.C.E. through ancient Greece, Roman times, the sixteenth through eighteenth centuries, and the influence of Queen Amalia on clothing of the 1800s. In a nontechnical yet authoritative style, Mavromatis seamlessly weaves together fashion and history. Did you know that Minoan women were the first to war hats? They wore two kinds—one looked like "inverted pots" and the other resembled berets.

Louisiana State Museum

http://www.crt.state.la.us/crt/museum/lsmnet3.htm

The Louisiana State Museum presents *Elegance After Dark: Evening Wear in Louisiana from 1896 to 1996,* an online exhibit that shows fashion in the context of social changes and the "unique joie de vivre" of the state. Beginning in 1896, the exhibit reflects the dress of the southern belle era, the Jazz Age (1920–1930), the period from 1930 to 1946, and the modern century (1946–1964), and concludes with the era of power and opulence (1980–1996).

GEMOLOGY

Greek Jewelry—5000 Years of Tradition

http://www.addgr.com/jewel/elka/index.html

The Hellenic Silver and Goldsmith Centre presents a history of Greece from Hellenic civilization to modern times. By explaining both the styles and techniques goldsmiths and jewelers used, the tour helps illuminate both the history and culture of pre-Hellenic and Hellenic civilization.

World of Gems

http://www.tradeshop.com/gems/index.html

Students and teachers interested in the lapidary arts should not miss this field trip. A certified gemologist explains how gems are classified, cut and polished, enhanced, weighed, and cared for. There are many photographs, as well as much consumer information. For example, you will learn whether gems are good investments and how to tell fakes from real gems.

MOBILES AND KINETIC SCULPTURES

http://brand.www.media.mit.edu/people/brand/mobiles.html

Remember John Henry's battle with the steam shovel? Now your students can observe a battle between a human artist and a computer as they design mobiles and kinetic sculptures. Matthew Brand, a scientist at the Media Lab at the Massachusetts Institute of Technology, presents this exhibit on kinetic mobiles, which actually move on screen. He takes you step-by-step through both the human and artificial intelligence processes of examining an actual object such as a horse and eventually rendering it into an abstract mobile. Along the way, students will gain an understanding and perhaps an appreciation of all nonrepresentational art, artificial intelligence, and the works of Alexander Calder.

PHOTOGRAPHY

Eadweard James Muybridge

http://linder.com/muybridge

Did you know that the first motion picture was the result of an argument about horses? In the 1850s, Governor Leland Stanford of California asked the renowned photographer Eadweard Muybridge to settle an argument about whether all four hooves of a galloping horse left the ground at once. In order to determine whether horses did indeed "fly," Muybridge created the sequential image and projected it onto a screen through a device he called a zoopraxiscope. Although administrators fail to answer the question about the horse, they present an honest portrayal of the eccentric artist (known as the father of motion pictures) and his works, accompanied by music from the silent film era. Because much of Muybridge's work involved nude men and women, you may wish to check the site before you take your students.

International Center of Photography

http://www.icp.org

The collections of the International Center of Photography preserve, interpret, and honor twentieth-century photography, with an emphasis on photojournalism and documentary photography. During our last tour, the site featured the works of David Seymour, who documented the economic and social conditions of France's workers in 1933, the Spanish Civil War, 1947 Germany, 1950 Italy, and 1954 Greece and Germany. We also toured *Weegee's World* and learned about Arthur Fellig, who perfected tabloid news photography. The tour covers Fellig's career from his work for ACME News (he was the first to be grated permission to monitor police radios) to his abstract manipulated photographs.

Museum of Photographic Arts

http://www.mopa.org/exhibition.html

San Diego's Museum of Photographic Arts is one of the oldest photographic museums in the United States, but it doesn't rest of its laurels. Every year, it features six to eight different exhibitions, many of which are available for virtual field trips. The exhibitions range from individual photographers to topics such as *Seascapes* or *Feeling the Spirit: Searching the World for the People of Africa*. Teachers may want to take a trip in advance and download the teacher's guide for the current main exhibition, which features background information and suggested classroom activities.

CHAPTER 7

LANGUAGE AND PERFORMING ARTS

Our literature field trips go from Appalachia to Shakespeare, with a detour to Camelot. Students can learn about international music from Quincy Jones, tour Carnegie Hall, pay a visit to 1940s Harlem, and listen to some of the world's greatest poets.

 ## LANGUAGE ARTS AND LITERATURE

Alcott, Louisa May

See Chapter 12—Alcott, Louisa May.

Blume, Judy

See Chapter 12—Blume, Judy.

Brett, Jan

See Chapter 12—Brett, Jan.

The Camelot Project

http://www.lib.rochester.edu/camelot/cphome.stm

Meet all the knights, ladies, heroes, and villains of Arthurian legend. The Camelot Project, sponsored by the University of Rochester's Robbins Library, includes Arthurian lore, text, and images as well as a bibliography. The materials are accessible by topic, author, or artist. We discovered that Morgan Le Fey, who's always received bad press, also had a reputation as a healer.

Dr. Seuss

See Chapter 12—Seuss, Dr.

Fitzgerald, F. Scott

See Chapter 12—Fitzgerald, F. Scott.

Internet Poetry Archive

http://www.sunsite.unc.edu/dykki/poetry

Internet Poetry Archive is a collaboration between the University of North Carolina Press and the University's Office of Internet Technology. Administrators of this site want to make poetry accessible to teachers and students by teaching new ways of presenting and studying poets and their works. At the time of publication, the site featured Philip Levine, Robert Pinsky, and Nobel Prize winners Seamus Heaney and Czeslaw Milosz. Students will gain a greater appreciation of poetry by listing to audio clips of the poets reading their works. There are photographs and other graphics that aid in understanding the poems.

Little House on the Prairie

http://www.vvv.com/~jenslegg

Jennifer Slegg, a Laura Ingalls Wilder fan, will introduce you to the famous author and her family. Although you have to pick your way through the commercials and advertising as carefully as if you are skipping through fields of tender young wheat, the summaries of Wilder's books, the story-writing contest for children of all ages, the information on Wilder, and the activities make it worth the visit. Your students can learn to churn butter and grind wheat by hand—but you had better warn them that it took Wilder all day to grind enough wheat to make flour for one loaf of bread.

Minds-Eye Monster Project

http://www.win4edu.com/minds-eye/center.html

Your class can choose a school anywhere in the world for this "monstrous" collaboration designed to enhance reading comprehension and process writing. Students draw a monster and describe their creation in an e-mail message sent to the partner school, where students will then try to redraw the original monster. At the conclusion of the collaboration, both sketches are posted on-site so students can see how the two monsters compare. Should you choose to participate, simply fill out the registration form on-site, and a list of potential partner schools will be given to you. There are explanations and helpful hints on how to make the collaboration successful.

The Moonlit Road

http://www.themoonlitroad.com/welcome001.html

Light your lantern, enter the gate, and wander through the moonlit back roads of the South. Enter the storytellers' cabins and listen to people like Cajun J. J. Reneaux as they share local tales such as *Marie Jolie*. Each month, new stories are featured, and prior stories are archived on-site. Your students can learn about the unique Creole language known as Gullah or the coal mining culture of Kentucky. Tell them to pay attention, or they might find themselves married to a Georgian "boo-hog."

Native American Folktales

See Chapter 1—Native Americans—Cherokee Tribe.

Shakespeare

http://the-tech.mit.edu/Shakespeare/works.html

The complete works of William Shakespeare are available at this site. The works are arranged categorically, by tragedy, comedy, history, and poetry.

Theodore Tugboat

http://www.cochran.com/theodore

Theodore Tugboat is known throughout Canada as the friendliest tugboat in the world. He'd love to spend some time with you and introduce you to his friends Emily the Vigorous; George the Valiant (he's rather impatient and believes any challenge can be solved by his size and power); Foduck the Vigilant (a reliable source of technical knowledge); and Hank, the smallest tugboat. Theodore would like you to help him with his interactive stories. He needs help deciding whether to visit his friend Barrington Barge or welcome a big ship to the harbor that he has never seen before. There is also an online coloring book and an audio story on-site.

Worldwide Words

http://www.quinion.com/words

Ask your students whether they would rather share a meal with a quidnunc or a deipnosophist. They will be able to answer after spending some time at this site. Michael Quinion, who describes himself as "the only lexicographer programming interpreter in captivity," will spend time with your students deciphering new words as well as the origins and true meanings of existing words. Each week, the site features at least one new short article with an extended definition of a new word, such as co-opetition (essentially a judicious mix of competition and cooperation). There are also articles about the English language covering a variety of topics, such as the distinction between an engine and a motor or the origin of words for colors. By the way, your students' choices will depend upon whether they prefer to spend their time with gossips or masters of dinner table conversations.

MOTION PICTURE INDUSTRY
http://library.advanced.org/10015

When you mention going to a film studio, most people think of a tour of Universal Studios. But thanks to three film students, now you can take your class through the process of writing a script, casting, choosing camera shots, and adding sound effects while trying to stay within a budget. Unlike real movie-making, the forced multiple choice format for decision making keeps the project under control. There are also interviews with people in the film industry and reference materials such as a glossary of movie terms. Perhaps one of your students will become the next Louis B. Mayer!

MUSIC AND RADIO

Canadian Broadcasting Corporation
http://www.cbc4kids.ca

Tune in to the Canadian Broadcasting Corporation's site, where your students can learn to produce their own radio dramas. Hosts will take them through the process of scriptwriting and the creation of sound effects. They will be able to tour the company's drama studio and learn how the sounds of a train, wind, marching feet, and the like are created. While they are there, they may want to check out the Canadian and international best-seller lists or learn about classical music.

For other information contained in this site, see Chapter 10—General Science—Canadian Broadcasting Corporation.

Experience Music Project
http://www.experience.org/hilow.asp

Ready to rock and roll? Take an interactive journey through the history of the "Seattle sound," courtesy of the Experience Music Museum. Several modern bands with Seattle roots such as Nirvana and Pearl Jam are profiled, and various artists will discuss their influences, some of which may surprise your students. For example, Dick Dale discusses Gene Krupa's influence on his surf guitar sound, and Bootsy Collins discusses James Jamerson's effect on his bass playing. There is also a guitar and bass exhibit, which spans the 1932 Dobro, 1935 Audiovox, 1954 Stratocaster, and the 1953 Gibson Electric. Students can see view the various instruments and their specifications and hear sound clips. There is an extensive section devoted to Jimi Hendrix, including excerpts from his songs and diary.

Great Day in Harlem

http://www.harlem.org/greatday.html

In 1958, Art Kane, a photographer for *Esquire*, conceived a group photograph that would bring together the most important people in the field of jazz. Jean Bach brought the 57- person portrait to life in 1954 in a documentary of reminiscences by these jazz greats. Students can either click on any of the people in the photographs or search the materials by name or instrument. Photographs, quotes, and brief biographical materials are available for such popular greats as Count Basie and Dizzy Gillespie; and musicians such as Red Allen, the New Orleans trumpeter known for his rhythmic "womping"; and for tenor saxophone player Lester Young.

Guitars

http://www.si.edu/organiza/museums/nmah/lemel/guitars

This tour is certain to hold the interest of any teenager! The exhibit, *From Frying Pan to Flying V: The Rise of the Electric Guitar,* sponsored by the Lemelson Center for the Study of Invention and Innovation at the National Museum of American History, shows how the guitar was combined with the pickup and amplifier to create a new instrument and sound that profoundly changed popular music in the twentieth century. Through profiles of inventors such as Leo Fender (developer of the Stratocaster and Telecaster) and performers such as Chuck Berry, Jimi Hendrix, the Rolling Stones, Bonnie Raitt, and Prince, the exhibit stresses the importance of the interaction among inventors, merchants, musicians, luthiers, engineers, scholars, and connoisseurs. Students can see such guitars as a Martin steel-stringed acoustic or Junior Brown's guit-steel. In addition to merely admiring the cool looks, students can actually learn how guitars work.

New Orleans Musicians

See Chapter 3—United States—Louisiana—New Orleans.

Qradio

http://commerce2.qradio.net/default.htm

Imagine walking into an international music store and meeting Quincy Jones. Jones has established Qradio to bring worldwide music to the Internet. Focusing on South Africa, Brazil, and Cuba, he provides sound bites, background, and news from the international music world. Choose a country or type of music ranging from jazz to hip-hop to African choral. Jones provides an intelligent, basic overview of different kinds of music and of course an opportunity to buy whatever you like—we told you this was a music store.

THEATERS AND PLAYS

Ancient Greek and Roman Stagecraft

http://didaskalia.berkeley.edu

Learn about the theater and stagecraft of ancient times, including actors, masks, costumes, and sets. The tour begins in the Theater of Dionysus in Athens, where, according to legend, a man named Thespis first had the idea to add speaking actors to performances. There are three-dimensional reconstructions of the sixth-century B.C.E. theater and the development of the odeion designed by Pericles. Tour the facility while meeting the players and dramatists such as Aeschylus, Sophocles, and Euripides. There are also three-dimensional reconstructions of the life masks used in performances. If you have time, tour some of the other theatrical buildings around Greece and Rome. Maps are provided so you won't lose your way.

Carnegie Hall

http://www.carnegiehall.org/visit/index.html

Now your students can tour Carnegie Hall from the entrance to back-stage . . . or from its original opening performance—when notables paid $1 to $2 for a five-day concert to hear the Symphony and Oratorio Society under the direction of someone named Peter Ilyich Tchaikovsky—to the present. They can see original drawings, photographs, and concert programs and hear actual voices of some of the great performers, such as Nellie Melba (the Australian soprano who inspired melba toast and peach melba) and Isaac Stern. What's Carnegie Hall without a spectacle? Students can view a photo bubble that allows a 360-degree view of the hall. And they will be met at the door by a very important person: Gino Francesconi, the Carnegie Hall archivist.

Japanese Noh Theater

http://www.enncorp.co.jp/Exhibit/noh/home.html

Noh, Japan's oldest form of theater, became a popular form of entertainment for the fourteenth-century warrior. This site gives a brief history of the theater and masks with several photographs. Students will even be able to meet Masuda Houshun, a Noh artisan, and his family. The Noh masks, which seem rigid, actually convey emotions, which are expressed by a slight change in the mask's angle, the reflection of light, the *utai* (dramatic chant) and the *hayashi* (the accompaniment of drums and flutes).

Tower Lyrics Archive

http://www.ccs.neu.edu/home/tower/lyrics.html

This site is an invaluable source for lyrics for many of the songs in popular cultural plays and movies. At the current time, there are lyrics from the works of Andrew Lloyd Webber (*Cats, Evita,* and *Phantom of the Opera*), Alain Boubil and Claude Michel Schoenberg (*Les Misérables* and *Miss Saigon*), Gilbert and Sullivan, and Disney. There is also a miscellaneous section with lyrics from works that will appeal to older students, such as *Grease, Tommy,* and the *Rocky Horror Picture Show.*

CHAPTER 8

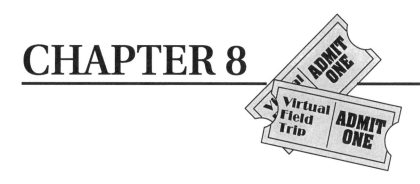

BUSINESS AND INDUSTRY

We can't persuade our local factory to let us take our children on a tour, but who needs them any more? On virtual field trips, classes can not only practice routing phone calls, take quizzes, and ask questions of leading experts in the field but can participate in processes that modern liability insurance requirements would never allow, such as oil drilling, international shipping, mining, and pencil manufacturing. Students will gain a more realistic perspective about money after a visit to the U.S. Treasury, two federal reserve banks, and the Social Security Administration, and afterward they can participate in the process of constructing a simulated national budget.

See also Chapter 1—U.S. History—Nineteenth-Century Industry.

ADVERTISING

CreatabiliToys

http://www.toymuseum.com

Students can gain an appreciation and understanding of the world of advertising at CreatabiliToys—a museum that holds a collection of more than 650 advertising icons spanning a century of U.S. history. Did you know that the lonely Maytag repairman is the most successful advertising character in the history of American television, that Herschel Bernardi was the voice of Charlie Tuna, and that creators of Speedy Alka Seltzer and his 30 different facial expressions used a filmmaking technique so secret that the tape was kept in a locked Hollywood studio vault? Your students can visit and learn the marketing reasoning behind Mr. Bubble, the Trix Rabbit, Sony Boy, and the Little Dutch Boy. Did you know that Elmer, Elsie the Cow's husband, became the head spokesman for Elmer's Glue in order to support the family when Beauregard was born?

Pez Museum

http://www.spectrumnet.com/pez/pezexhibit.html

In 1952, Pez—originally peppermint blocks developed in 1927 to help people quit smoking—conquered America. There are now more than 250 kinds of Pez dispensers, and a visit to the Burlingame, California, Pez Museum is like a walk through history. Your students can see the dispensers, which have reflected almost every cultural phenomenon of the United States, from clown whistles to Teenage Mutant Ninja Turtles.

INTERNATIONAL TRADE

http://www.apl.com/boomerangbox

This site is an excellent source for learning about international trade and regulations. Students can track the boomerang box cargo container as it travels from Seattle to Asia by ship, train, and truck. The American President Lines eagle is the tour guide, and he gets plenty of help from his company, the Port of Seattle, and Metropolitan King County. While learning about international trade, students will discover where the clothing they wear, the products they use, and the food they eat come from and how these items get to them. During the voyage, they will stop in many countries around the world and may be lucky enough to run into a few festivities, such as the Chinese New Year's celebration, along the way. There is a glossary of terms used in the international trade industry and links to various lesson plans. If you don't find what you need, ask the eagle. He'll be happy to answer your questions or set you up with a pen pal somewhere around the world.

Pencils

http://www.pencils.com

Did you ever wonder how pencils are made? Take this tour and follow the development of the modern pencil from the discovery of graphite to modern manufacturing techniques. You will even learn why most pencils are yellow. Quite a few famous people have depended on this simple instrument—John Steinbeck used more than 60 pencils per day to write his novels. Henry David Thoreau wouldn't think of using anything else—his father owned a pencil factory where young Henry worked before writing *Walden*. In fact, the company's products had the reputation of being the hardest, blackest pencils in the United States. Follow the *Great Eraser Caper* and learn how they are put on pencils, how they are made, and who makes them—you rarely find erasers on pencils in Europe.

MANUFACTURING—AUTOMOBILES

Blackhawk Automotive Museum

http://blackhawkauto.org

The Blackhawk Automotive Museum, affiliated with the University of California at Berkeley, provides this tour of automotive engineering and the automobile's connection with the history, lifestyles, fashion, and culture of twentieth-century America. You will learn, for example, how the fire that destroyed Olds Motor Works in 1901 is actually considered one of the best things to happen to the automotive industry because it resulted in the implementation of mass production techniques by Ransom Olds. Students can see photographs and specifications of 12 landmark cars, as well as a history of their development and developers. There's even an art collection of vintage model gas stations, toys, and paintings by artists such as Henry Ebby and Jules Dalou, including the famous painting of Father Time handing over his hourglass to the triumphant Demogeot, who set a speed record by covering 2 miles in 58.8 seconds.

Sloan Automotive Museum

http://aristotle.sils.umich.edu/exhibit/sloan/sloan.html

Wander through the galleries at the Sloan Museum to learn the history of the automobile industry in Flint, Michigan, the birthplace of General Motors (GM). Two tours are available. The car gallery has a collection ranging from the 1902 Flint Roadster to the 1983 Buick Riviera pace car. The *Tour of Historic Car Making* begins with the Flint Wagon Works Carriage Company in 1908 and covers the transition between the carriage and the automobile. Students see photographs of horses and automobiles sharing the same roads and learn how advertising and other factors displaced the horse and carriage. The presentation covers both the negatives and positives of the automobile, including traffic jams, early "human traffic lights," and working conditions in the first GM plant, built in 1908. They will also learn how Alfred B. Sloan started managing production and organized GM into divisions and how his techniques were adopted by large companies worldwide.

MINING AND NATURAL RESOURCE MANAGEMENT

See also Chapter 3—United States—Wyoming—Sunflower Elementary School.

Coal Mining

http://www.osmre.gov/learn.htm

The Office of Surface Mining of the U.S. Department of Labor presents *The Learning Gateway*, a series of educational pages designed for high school students. The site deals with coal mining and its regulations under the Surface Mining Law. The materials are primarily multiple choice quizzes that are immediately graded on-site. Topics cover locations of coal seams, its uses, mining procedures, environmental procedures and regulations, and reclamation procedures. There are also coloring books, crossword puzzles, and games.

Mineral Management Service of Alaska

http://www.mms.gov/alaska/kids

The Mineral Management Service (MMS) of Alaska will tell your students all about crude oil, off-shore drilling, and exploration. After taking this trip, they will know all about jack-ups and drill ships, oil spill emergency response preparedness, and even how an ice island is constructed. It gets very cold, so be sure to dress properly. In fact, although in most parts of the world drilling platforms are constructed of steel, it's so cold in the Arctic that seawater is used to build them. The MMS has a lot of responsibilities, one of which is to monitor and protect the bowhead whale, which is essential to the Inuits' survival. Richard Pomeroy of the MMS will be more than happy to take you along on an airplane ride as he conducts his annual aerial whale survey. There is also an experiment illustrating the principles of ballast and stability.

Museum of Science and Industry

http://www.msichicago.org/info/infohome.html

Cliff, the manager of the Museum of Science and Industry's coal mine, will take your students on a tour of a simulated working mine. Tell them to hang on carefully while the cage descends to the bottom of the mine at a rate of 600 feet per minute. They will be traveling far down to the bowels of the earth—it's like having a 60-story building of solid rock over their heads. Students will learn why miners don't look directly at each other while they speak, how the foreman checks for methane in the safety room (there are now a lot of unemployed canaries), how roof bolters are used to prevent collapse, and how today's techniques differ from those used in the 1930s.

For other materials contained in this site, see Chapter 10—General Science—Museum of Science and Industry.

MONEY, BANKING, AND ECONOMICS

Currency

http://woodrow.mpls.frb.fed.us/econed/curric/money.html

The Federal Reserve Bank of Minneapolis will show your students how money is printed and how to detect counterfeit currency, explain the role of the Federal Reserve Bank (a.k.a. the bank for banks), and present the history of money from ancient bartering to precious metals to coins and paper currency. Most of the unit focuses on paper currency, which makes up about 95 percent of U.S. money. Teachers will appreciate the review questions and study guide.

Federal Reserve Bank

http://www.frbsf.org/econedu/games

The Federal Reserve Bank of San Francisco will take your students on a treasure hunt that provides an excellent background on economic theories. Students will journey through the *Great Economic Timeline* gathering answers that will enable them to unlock an ancient treasure chest. Along the way they will meet ten of the greatest economists from Adam Smith (1723–1791) to Irving Fisher (1867–1947), who will tell them about the physiocratic, classical, Marxist, marginalist, institutionalist, and Keynesian schools of economic theory. Play the computerized simulation to discover how fiscal policies affect a nation's economy. Players make policy decisions and see how they affect inflation and unemployment. Federal Reserve economists are available to answer questions via e-mail.

For other materials available at this site, see Chapter 1—U.S. History—Federal Reserve Bank—American Currency Exhibit.

National Budget Simulation

http://garnet.berkeley.edu:3333/budget/budget.html

It isn't as easy to balance the national budget as your students might think. They can gain firsthand knowledge of the process and the trade-offs that have to be made by playing the *National Budget Simulation,* courtesy of the Center for Community Economic Research at the University of California at Berkeley. It was interesting to note how cuts in certain programs result in little additional revenue. Both long and short versions of the game are available. If you have questions, the site links to the current budget and other sources of economic information. Administrators will be adding an additional feature in the near future—students who successfully balance the budget can submit their work to the site. All successful budgets will be averaged and a composite "Internet" budget will be produced.

Social Security Administration

http://www.ssa.gov/kids/index.htm

There are two tours available at the Social Security Administration—one for younger students and one for teens. The first is conducted by some of the administration's friends from the animal kingdom and presents an elementary overview of Social Security and why it exists. The tour geared towards older students has much more practical and relevant information, including how to apply for a card, the history of Social Security and how it works, and why it is necessary. In order to keep students' interest, quizzes, puzzles, and anecdotes are included, such as the story of the first Social Security card and the lowest number (they are not the same) and the story of the most unusual Social Security card in history and how an advertising campaign by Woolworth's adversely affected the life of one Ms. Xxxxx.

U.S. Treasury

http://www.treas.gov/kids

The U.S. Treasury Department and Trez the cat will help teach your students about currency, savings, and taxes. Be sure to visit *Lemonade Stand,* where students can start their own virtual lemonade stand, lawn-mowing service, or band, and learn how and why people pay taxes. We had a great time with our band, "Complexity," from hiring a singer to playing our first gig. Other tours include an explanation of savings bonds, the minting and printing of currency, counterfeit currency, and a history of the Treasury Department and its branches, including the Secret Service. Younger students will enjoy playing *Face Flips,* (a currency recognition game), *Find the Fifty,* and *Count the Cash*—designed to enhance their counting skills. Trez will also take you on a tour of the Treasury building and even show you the actual door to the vault. There isn't much in the teacher resources section beyond an art activity for making your own money.

NEWSPAPERS AND MAGAZINES

Time Magazine for Kids

http://www.pathfinder.com/tfk

Time-Warner hosts an online version of *Time for Kids* with news, cartoons, and feature stories from the print edition. Children can write letters to the editor via e-mail or participate in votes on such issues as whether or not life exists on other planets or whether advertisements should be allowed in school. Visit the multimedia center for interactive activities. In the past, children have been able to build their own onscreen robots or take a trip in the *Mars Time Machine.* This site is also a good source for research because there is an archive of past issues, searchable by date or topic.

Weekly Reader

http://www.weeklyreader.com

Not only can students in grades K to 6 check out articles and features from each week's *Weekly Reader,* but they can also go on the field trip of the month. Past field trips have included a trip backstage to the Grammy Awards. Each field trip makes use of the Internet in a way the print maga-zine can't. During the Grammy trip, for example, students had an oppor-tunity to hear a mystery musical instrument and e-mail in their guess. They can also e-mail letters to authors and comments about other articles, as well as participate in e-mail polls. As with the print magazine, there is some relatively low-key advertising.The site also has a separate teacher and parent section, bu the material seemed identical to that in the students' sections.

TECHNOLOGY

AT&T Labs

http://www.att.com/attlabs/brainspin

AT&T labs has produced this tour in conjunction with *Highways, Hubs, and Networks,* a technology curriculum developed in cooperation with Scholastic. At the current time, four modules are featured, with more planned. Through interactive activities, students can follow the communications industry from development of the first telephone number to the Internet. In the *Numbers Game,* they will learn that telephone numbers originated as the result of an 1879 measles epidemic (find out why phone companies were afraid to use numbers before the epidemic). They will then use math to learn how to calculate how many phone numbers are possible with the current system and when specific plans will run out of numbers. In addition to the unit one might expect on Alexander Graham Bell, students can *Take a Ride on the Infobahn* where they might run into traffic jams or wide-open freeways. During the ride they will learn about the past, present, and future of the Internet and how different types of information require various methods of access. They can also try their hand at routing calls throughout the country using computerized switching techniques and try to keep the network running smoothly.

CHAPTER 9

MATHEMATICS AND LOGIC

Give students math workbooks or write equations on the blackboard, and their eyes may immediately glaze over. Take them on some of our virtual math and logic field trips and turn them loose on everything from elementary counting exercises to tangrams and Gauss distributions, and you will have to tear them away. They can use math to fly airplanes, wander through labyrinths, work cash registers, and meet some of the greatest mathematicians in the history of the world. We even have a field trip especially for physically challenged students.

ABACUS
http://www.ee.ryerson.ca:8080/~elf/abacus/

Now you can use the latest computer technology to teach students about the ancient abacus. In fact, L. Fernandes, from the Department of Electrical and Computer Engineering at Ryerson Polytechnic University of Toronto, seems to prefer the abacus. He relates the famous 1946 contest between the abacus and the electronic calculating machine in which "new technology" suffered quite a defeat. Ferdandes provides an interactive abacus, on which beads may be moved through the click of a mouse. The only concession he has made to technology is that, unlike a real abacus, the numeric value for each column is constantly shown and updated as students manipulate the beads. He will show you how to perform addition, subtraction, multiplication, and division and provide detailed illustrated instructions for building a Lego abacus, or *soroban* as it is known in Japan.

CALCULATING MACHINES
http://www.webcom.com/calc

Sometimes students fail to realize how modern technology has simplified their lives. Let them try to operate the 1885 Felt and Tarrant Comptometer at this site, which displays and discusses adding and calculating machines of the past. Students are able to view machines from the ancient abacus to the slide rule to Blaise Pascal's 1642 invention. Be sure to check the print advertisements that date from 1937 to 1954.

CAPTAIN ZOOM'S MATH ADVENTURE
http://www.af.mil/aflinkjr/entrance.htm

Younger students won't want to miss *Captain Zoom's Math Adventure,* sponsored by the U.S. Air Force. As junior members of the Air Force, students gather supplies to fly to a space station. They are given a lot of responsibility during this mission and have to decide how many supplies are needed and how they should be packed and distributed using basic math equations.

For other materials contained in this site, see Chapter 1—Military History—United States Air Force.

GAMES
http://www.funbrain.com

Geared toward elementary grades, the games at this site allow students to practice math facts while working at their own speed. Basic addition, subtraction, multiplication, and division are covered. In *Math Baseball,* the computer gives you a math problem. If you get the correct answer, the graphical baseball field tracks your singles, doubles, triples, and home runs (based on the level of difficulty of the question). Levels of difficulty range from easy to "braniac" (not much more complicated than 80 x 82). The *Cash Register Game* gives you the amount of a sale and the amount paid. It's up to you how to make the change as you enter amounts under various currency levels. Stay away from *Wacky Tales.* It's a lot like a worldwide group game of *Mad Libs* and is not well controlled. It accepts any word the student chooses to enter as long as it's correctly classified as a noun, adverb, or adjective.

MATH ONLINE
http://www.univie.ac.at/future.media/moe

Faculty from the University of Vienna in Austria invites middle school, high school, and university students to their *Math Online Gallery* for an interactive mathematical experience. Students will find multimedia learning units on such topics as plane and coordinate systems, quantum equations, analytical geometry, trigonometric functions, the Gauss distribution, and probability and statistics. Tools such as calculators, integrators, and function plotters are available on-site.

MATH TRADING CARDS
http://www.bulletproof.org/

Perhaps math trading cards will take the place of pop culture trading cards. Edmund Robertson, head of the Department of Mathematical and Computational Services at St. Andrew's University in Scotland, presents over 25 math trading cards. Each card has a portrait of a mathematician on the front and statistics and a biography on the back. Robertson has collected the greatest math team of all time, including such stars as Pythagoras, Omar Khayyám, Maria Agnesi (noted for her work in differential calculus and the first woman to chair a math department), and Karl Weierstrass, best known for his construction of the theory of complex functions.

MATHEMATICIANS
http://www.sci.hkbu.edu.hk/scilab/math/math.html

Morris Law, from the Faculty of Science at Hong Kong Baptist University, will introduce your students to 14 of the world's greatest seventeenth- to twentieth-century mathematicians. In addition to the more famous Blaise Pascal, Isaac Newton, and Albert Einstein, less familiar mathematicians include Charles Babbage, whose theorems form the basis of the modern electronic computer; Augustin-Louis Cauchy, who pioneered the study of analysis and the theory of permutation groups; and Carl Friedrich Gauss, who developed the first proof of the fundamental theory of algebra.

PLANE MATH
http://www.planemath.com

The goal of *Plane Math* is to encourage physically disabled fourth- to seventh-grade students to pursue aeronautics careers through the use of math problems provided over the Internet. The project, funded by the National Air and Space Administration (NASA), comprises three groups of interactive activities, each geared toward a different grade level. Each group of activities includes practical math problems, a career page featuring an interview with a disabled person in the aeronautics industry who can serve as a role model, a teacher/parent page with math topics and further activities, and material lists.

THE PUZZLING PLAYGROUND
http://playground.idtv.nl/speel/indexeng.htm

This playground, hosted by a Dutch media company, is full of interactive puzzles, games, and problems, including numbers, labyrinths, tangrams, and peg solitaire. Try to work Rubik's cube or solve some of the many riddles and paradoxes presented on-site. There is a special section for children under ten, and children who get stuck can always ask the

Puzzle Sphinx for help. When we had some trouble figuring out what "passes before the sun and makes no shadow," the Sphinx politely informed us that it was "air."

QUANDARIES AND QUERIES
http://MathCentral.uregina.ca/QQ/index.html

A high school teacher wants some "real life" examples of complex numbers that she can share with her students. An elementary student wonders why "lb." is the abbreviation for pound. Eric Cote, a seventh-grade student, wants to know "why the grade 6 math books tell you that the little number at the top right of another number is called the power, but the grade 7 and up books tell you it's called the exponent." *Quandaries and Queries,* sponsored by the University of Regina in Canada, has the answers. Website administrators invite any teacher or student to submit questions that they promise they will make every attempt to answer. Previous questions and answers are archived on-site, filed by grade level, although you might be surprised at some of the questions the elementary students have asked. The answers are pitched to appropriate grade levels. For example, administrators diplomatically explained to Eric the difference between five to the fourth power and the fourth power of five, while admitting that sometimes textbooks are very confusing.

CHAPTER 10

SCIENCE

Watch your mad scientists learn about cartography and satellite imagery as they shrink lakes and expand deserts. They can practice their genetics by creating monster flies, conduct forensic examinations, and analyze their own drinking water. Take them into outer space, on daring solo flights across the ocean, and inside human bodies. By the time you are through, Miss Frizzle's magic school bus will seem like a Model T.

ANATOMY

The Human Body

http://www.innerbody.com/indexbody.html

Informative Graphics, a company that produces software for technological viewing, will take your students on a trip through the ten systems of the human body, complete with animation. More than 100 illustrations and clear, relatively nontechnical texts are organized so that students can take either a self-guided or structured tour. For example, students can find out about the brain by going to either the central nervous system or the skull.

The Senses

http://www.hhmi.org/senses

The Howard Hughes Medical Institute provides this journey into the world of the senses and nervous system. Students will learn about the five senses and how the brain processes and perceives information accumulated through vision, hearing, taste, touch, and scent. There are optical illusions that show how the brain makes assumptions and how it senses change in the environment, a detailed section on how and why we see color, and images of the brain at work, including an explanation of modern brain-imaging techniques.

ARCHAEOLOGY

Backyard Dig

http://www.vetc.vsc.edu/ws/archeology/arch.htm

Nine-year-old Ryon produced this site as his report on a fifth- and sixth-grade project he participated in with his classmates from Westford Elementary School in rural Vermont. The students laid a metric grid over a site in their school's yard, excavated test pits, washed and catalogued artifacts, and produced a report. According to Ryon, "We were not just students, but junior scientists on a team." Your students can follow the step-by-step processes of searching fields for artifacts or constructing topographic maps. We guarantee that after this virtual trip, there are going to be some holes in the schoolyard.

Virtual Archaeology

http://ted.educ.sfu.ca/people/staff/jmd/archaeology/IntroPg.htm

Administrators of this site would like to take your students on an archaeological dig, during which they will engage in inventory surveys, testing, stratigraphy, and field writing. Students will be making the same decisions and asking themselves the same questions that archaeologists face on a daily basis. Each choice they make can be compared with those made by other students throughout the world as well as with those made by archaeological experts. If you run into any problems during your trip, archaeologists will be available to answer questions via e-mail.

AVIATION AND AEROSPACE

See also Chapter 1—Military History—United States Air Force *and* Chapter 12—Earhart, Amelia.

Flight

http://www.worldflight.org

Students are able to follow pilot Linda Finch as she recreates Amelia Earhart's flight around the world. While joining Finch on her 26,000-plus-nautical-mile trip, students will learn such concepts as the four forces of lift, gravity, thrust, and drag as expressed in Newton's Third Law of Motion. If you don't have time to take the entire trip, you can check Finch's daily flight logs or simply join in the numerous hands-on activities offered on-site. There is a separate teaching area with guides and resources. This site is sponsored by Pratt and Whitney, a division of United Technologies Corporation.

Invention of the Airplane

http://hawaii.cogsci.uiuc.edu/invent/air_main.shtml

Gary Bradshaw, a professor at the University of Illinois who studies psychology and aviation, has created a virtual museum that covers the invention and earliest days of the airplane. The tour begins with the quote, "To invent an airplane is nothing; to build an airplane is something; to fly an airplane is everything." Watching old movies of the earliest airplanes, viewing three-dimensional models, and even having the opportunity to fly a 1903 Wright brothers simulator, your students will come closer to the experience than they ever have. Bradshaw also has a short essay on the Wright brothers and a database of approximately 50 of the earliest airplanes from around the world.

BIOLOGY, CHEMISTRY, AND GENETICS

Chemical Carousel

http://library.advanced.org/11226/index.htm

Hop on board the *Chemical Carousel* for a trip around the carbon cycle, hosted by Captain Carbon. The Captain's days are rather full, what with defending atoms and saving the world from cubic zirconia, but he still has time to teach your students about the nature of the carbon cycle and its relationship to the processes of photosynthesis, digestion, combustion, and even the decomposition of the human body. The tour, designed for junior high and high school students and developed by three undergraduates at the University of North Carolina, integrates chemistry and biology and takes Captain Carbon inside things such as cereal and grass. Finally, he enters his greatest, final adventure, with his last words: "Whew!! It sure is hot in here. I'm burning up .. literally. All this combustion releases lots of heat. As soon as I hit my flash point, I'll combust too. Then I'll be off into the atmosphere with some oxygen as Carbon Dioxide, CO^2."

Cytogenetics Gallery

http://www.pathology.washington.edu/Cytogallery

High school biology students will want to pay a visit to the *Cytogenetics Gallery* to learn about chromosomes and chromosome abnormalities. The Department of Pathology at the University of Washington at Seattle will show them what chromosomes look like under a microscope and how abnormalities are identified. There is also an easy-to-understand section explaining the basics of chromosomes.

Genetic Engineering

http://www.kadets.d20.co.edu/~lundberg

Doug Lundberg, a science teacher at Air Academy High School in Colorado, teaches a year-long class devoted to laboratory research in plant tissue culture and recombinant DNA, and he's eager to share some of the genetic engineering activities, lesson plans, and experiments that he's developed. He'll show your students how to "capture a bit of immortality" by teaching them how to prepare, develop, stain, and karyotype their own chromosomes. (They have to be willing to draw some of their own blood. Squeamish students may prefer to use the DNA procedure at the University of Chicago's Allele Database Lab, described in this chapter.) Lundberg also provides pictures of DNA, includes a pictorial survey of the American Eugenics Movement, shares information on genetic engineering, and describes some of the practical uses of DNA testing.

Genetic Testing

http://www.gene.com/ae/AE/AEPC/NIH/index.html

Understanding Genetic Testing is a joint effort of the National Cancer Institute and the National Center for Human Genome Research to provide basic information about genetic testing and key genetic concepts. The site provides answers about the science of testing and its potential risks and benefits. An illustrated booklet describes what genes are, how they work, how they are linked to disease, and how genetic "mistakes" occur.

Molecular Modeling

http://www.nyu.edu/pages/mathmol

New York University (NYU) has designed this site to introduce your students to the field of molecular modeling and to illustrate, in a hands-on manner, its connection to mathematics. We suggest you start with the *Quick Tour* for introductory movies and discussions that will capture students' interest—perhaps one of them may be the one to discover the cure for cancer with this newfound knowledge. You might then want to pay a visit to the *Library of 3-D Molecular Structures*, to see pictures of molecules such as carbons, hydrocarbons, and amino acids. NYU has provided several K–12 activities that allow students to calculate the density of water and ice; review the concepts of mass, volume and density; and view photosynthetic molecular reactions. Be sure to check the *Hypermedia Textbooks* (grades 3–5 and 6–12), which include diagrams, analogies, and suggested activities. The 6–12-grade text even includes an online calculator.

Polymers

http://www.psrc.usm.edu/macrog

There is something of interest for all K–12 students at the *Macrogalleria*, managed by the Department of Polymer Science at the University of Mississippi. Students begin the tour by selecting a mall store they'd like to visit. Athletes may want to visit the sporting goods store, where they will see tennis rackets made of carbon fibers. Dissonance Records shows compact discs being made from polycarbonates. The second level of the *Macrogalleria, Up Close and Personal*, presents specific information on the polymer of your choice, with uses, the basics of its synthesis, and a three-dimensional rotatable model of a short chain. Other levels teach students the basic concepts of polymer physical chemistry, with each level containing more sophisticated concepts. For example, level five, entitled *Getting Polymers to Talk,* deals with molecular weight, polymer structure, thermal properties, instrument chemistry, and "wet chains."

University of Chicago's Student Allele Database Lab Bench

http://http.bsd.uchicago.edu/hgd-sad/LabBench

This project involves high school students in a long-term research project centered around a hands-on lab that allows them to produce a personal DNA "fingerprint." Students isolate their own DNA from cheek cells obtained from a mouthwash procedure. Samples are passed to the research center for processing, and photographs of the results are returned to the students so that they are able to determine their own genotypes. They have the option of submitting their results to the database, or they may perform "Hardy-Weinburg" calculations and statistical tests to compare their allelic frequencies to those in the database. As the database grows, students will be able to see the frequencies of this occurrence in divergent populations and see evidence for genetic drift and evolutionary patterns. The site also allows the analysis of data within the databank in which students can study a group of real or fictitious people and compare their genotypes to predictions, or compare two groups of real or fictitious people to each other to see how they differ.

Virtual Fly

http://vearthquake.calstatela.edu/edesktop/VirtApps/VflyLab/
IntroVflyLab.html

Virtual Fly, sponsored by faculty members and support staff at California State University, teaches the principle of genetic inheritance by allowing your students to play the role of a research geneticist. Students are able to virtually mate flies containing one or more genetic mutations and then see the characteristics of the offspring, which can also be mated. Based on the results, students can then determine the genetic rules they have applied.

BOTANY

The Great Plant Escape

http://www.urbanext.uiuc.edu/gpe

Detective Le Plant and his partners, Bud and Sprout, would like your students to help them solve the mysteries of plant life. This University of Illinois Cooperative Extension Service site allows your students to choose a case to solve, each of which includes a case history, clues, facts pertaining to the case, experiments, problems, and additional resource lists. The cases also include learning objectives. For example, in the *Search for Green Life,* students identify various parts of plants and their functions. The site, geared towards fourth- and fifth-grade students, includes a teacher's guide and incorporates math, science, the arts, and social studies. The detective also encourages students to submit questions via e-mail.

EARTH AND ENVIRONMENTAL EDUCATION

Biosphere 2

http://www.bio2.edu

Biosphere 2, once a notoriously flawed scientific experiment, is now managed by Columbia University and, in its reincarnation, has become a valuable learning and teaching tool for understanding environmental interactions. The 7,200,000-cubic-foot sealed glass structure contains seven wilderness ecosystems, including a rain forest, a 900,000-gallon ocean, a savanna, a marsh, and a desert. Researchers use the self-contained facility to examine how each biosphere will change as carbon dioxide and other substances accumulate in the atmosphere. Your students can tour the entire facility or study one or more specific environmental issues. They are able, for example, to operate and obtain data from more than 750 sensors located in the various environments and plot various data to study different hypotheses and processes such as photosynthesis.

California Energy Commission

http://www.energy.ca.gov/education

The California Energy Commission invites your students to take a trip down the *Renewable Road* and learn about alternative energy sources. Materials, geared toward all age groups, cover the energy created by biomass (otherwise inelegantly known as garbage), geothermal energy, hydroelectricity, the sun, and the wind. There are interesting and informative experiments and projects from which students can find out how much energy is in a peanut or use a lemon to make a voltaic battery capable of powering a digital watch. Be sure to read *Devoured in the Dark*, an interactive horror serial novel about three students who have to find answers in a world that has suddenly become dark. Perhaps students would prefer to learn through playing *Watt's That*, hosted by Flip Switch. *Poor Richard's Energy Almanac* compares energy use in 1740 and today, and *Super Scientists* has brief biographies of people instrumental in the field of energy from Anders Celsius to Granville T. Woods. People are invited to submit e-mail questions to California's energy experts.

Drinking Water

http://www.epa.gov/OGWDW/kids

The U.S. Environmental Protection Agency's Office of Ground Water and Drinking Water has compiled this site to teach children all about drinking water. Through games, experiments, and projects, students are able to follow a drop of water from its source to the final treatment process. The agency will show students how to build their own aquifers, how to see whether the water in their community is safe, and how the water treatment process works. Some of the materials are presented in Spanish.

Environmental Protection Agency

http://www.epa.gov/epahome/students.htm

The U.S. Environmental Protection Agency (EPA) has developed the *Student Center* for middle and high school students. Your class can spend hours learning about environmental issues, clubs, activities, careers, internships, and scholarships. The site is topically organized by conservation, ecosystems, water, human health, environmental basics, environmental club projects, and water. Each portion of the site is extensive, so we suggest students pick a specific topic of interest. For example, the section on conservation covers environmental stewardship; natural resources; pollution prevention; and the principles of energy, soil, and water conservation. The *Acid Rain Sourcebook* is a multimedia electronic textbook that includes experiments and activities. Ecosystems includes a tour of biomes and a visit to the research vessel *Lake Guardian,* the only nonpolluting research ship on the Great Lakes. The EPA has been kind enough to provide a *Teacher's Lounge,* where they will let you know about available K–12 resources, guides, curricula, and grants. Younger students (ages 5–12) will prefer the *EPA Kids Page* and its *Explorer Club,* where they may choose between the art, game, and science rooms. Materials include a comic book about a reporter who uncovers facts about the ozone layer, activity books, and puzzles and games. Be sure they pay a visit to Charlie Chipmunk, who will tell them what it's like to live in a park that becomes polluted.

Meteorology

http://www.earthwatch.com

Earth Watch Communications, the first company to develop three-dimensional weather visualization for the broadcast, film, and postproduction industries, lets your students create their own weather reports, complete with graphics. Students are able to find up-to-the-minute weather conditions throughout the world and procure displays of watches and warnings for every county in the United States. National weather forecasts, satellite images, and reports of current worldwide weather conditions are also available.

Rainbows

http://www.unidata.ucar.edu/staff/blynds/rnbw.html

Administrators of this site believe that rainbows are "one of the most spectacular light shows observed on earth" and want to teach your students all about this meteorological phenomenon. They trace the study of the rainbow back to René Descartes, who in 1637 simplified the explanation by using a water droplet and showing how it reacted to light falling on it (Descartes's illustrations are included). Students will learn how the various colors are formed, what makes a double rainbow, and what a supernumerary arc is. There are also experiments that can be performed in class.

Virtual Earthquake

http://vquake.calstatela.edu/edesktop/VirtApps/VirtualEarthQuake/
VquakeIntro.html

How would you like to become certified as a virtual seismologist? *Virtual Earthquake* allows your students to locate the epicenter and determine the Richter measurement of a hypothetical earthquake from recordings of seismic waves. Students make simple measurements on three seismograms provided on-site. Be sure to read the introductory materials, which explain earthquakes and how to use the materials on-site.

Visualizing Earth

http://visearth.ucsd.edu

"A picture is worth a thousand words, and a map is worth a thousand data points," say the administrators of the *Visualizing Earth Project*. The project was established for the purpose of promoting research in cognition and visualization, adapting existing geographical information systems (GIS) technology and data sources for ease of use in schools, and developing model curriculums at the middle school level. Using the latest information available from satellites and hosted by the University of San Diego, the project includes such notables as Dr. Eric Frost, Daniel Barstow (who also developed the ACCU-weather forecast), and astronaut Sally Ride. Students are able to explore the Aral Sea in Uzbekistan and Kazakstan and watch as it shrinks by 75 percent from its original size—the equivalent of draining Lakes Erie and Ontario. Students can enlarge and create three-dimensional images of satellite photos of San Diego and San Francisco and learn about fault lines by using photographs and animation. Did you know that the fault line along the Pacific and North American plates moves at approximately the same rate that fingernails grow? Watch as Dr. Eric Frost uses fig newtons to tell students about the layers of the earth. Or, learn how to use animal cookies to teach about tectonic plates and pop-up models to teach about volcanic eruptions, how and why the walls of Jericho keep tumbling down, and how to transfer three dimensions of information from a two-dimensional map. High school and junior high students will learn about isostasy, spatial visualization, earthquake creation, seismograph data interpretation, and much more.

Wisconsin Department of Natural Resources

http://www.dnr.state.wi.us/org/caer/ce/eek

This state agency provides EEK! (*Environmental Education for Kids*), an electronic magazine for grades 4–8. Information is provided about trees, wildlife, fish, air, water, and land. Department officials caution children that they "might even find stuff that helps with homework—ugh!" Students won't have to worry, however, because this section is clearly marked. Instead, they may want to engage in winter stargazing, go on a snow flea hunt (they will be hard to find because they are only 2 millimeters in size), or ice fish. State officials will prepare students for each of these activities as they carefully explain such things as environmental laws and how to dress to avoid hypothermia. The park ranger will even share his diary and answer any questions your students might have. If he gets too busy (he puts in very long days), you can visit with the wildlife biologist.

FORENSICS

http://forensicfiles.bc.sympatico.ca

Newton Beagle and the Center for the Promotion and Advancement of Science Education want your students to help solve an international heist of an endangered species. Students participate in a mock capture of poachers of endangered wildlife through hands-on experiments and activities that will make forensic science understandable and relevant.

GENERAL SCIENCE

Annenberg/Canadian Public Broadcasting Projects

http://www.learner.org/exhibits

The Annenberg/Canadian Public Broadcasting (CPC) project is dedicated to bringing multimedia education into the classroom. Each month, a new exhibit is added, and previously featured projects are archived on-site. Past projects have included units on garbage, medical ethics, volcanoes, and the physics of roller coasters. Future projects will include such topics as personality, earthquakes, weather, and space. Each unit includes texts, graphics, an extensive bibliography, and at least one interactive activity. For example, the unit on amusement park rides allows students to design their own roller coaster and see whether it passes a safety inspection. They will also learn how Newton's laws affect bumper car collisions. In the unit on medical ethics, students choose one of three real life scenarios (living with cancer, cloning, or handling headaches) and take part in the medical ethics decision-making process.

Ask Dr. Universe

http://www.wsu.edu/DrUniverse

Dr. W. S. Universe, from Washington State University, is living proof that the axiom "curiosity killed the cat" is simply not true. This cat is so curious, in fact, that she even wants to know what your students are thinking about. Send an e-mail to the doctor to learn exactly what a black hole is, why spiders don't stick to their own webs, or whether the chicken or the egg came first. The doctor posts new questions and answers daily, and hundreds of past Q&As are archived topically on-site. How does she do it? Dr. Universe has a lot of connections at Washington State University, and being a cat, she'll follow the university's researchers into the field, the library, the lab, or just about anywhere she needs to go to find answers. She'll even translate questions and answers into Spanish, French, German, or Italian. And her connections extend beyond the scientific community. Dr. Universe has answered questions about philosophy, economics, and a variety of other subjects.

Canadian Broadcasting Corporation

http://www.cbc4kids.ca

Pay a visit to *The Lab* at the Canadian Broadcasting Corporation for "weird news from the world of science," experiments, and in-depth features about various topics. News, contained within the section entitled *Planet Quirks*, presents information in the form of entertaining multiple choice quizzes. For example, possible correct responses to "why it may be hard for you to get up in the morning" include (1) "Dogs enjoy eating alarm clocks," (2) Children really like to hear their parents yell outside their door," and (3) "You're just not a morning person." Choosing the correct answer will yield scientific explanations. The experiments, which can be done at home, are presented in three parts—a question and explanation, instructions for the experiment, and a "Did you know?" section. Every week, a different scientific phenomenon is featured, and archives of past features are available. Features have included the "space race," El Nino, auditory illusions, and memory malfunctions. Bob McDonald, the host of the broadcast corporation's show, *Quirks and Quarks*, will share his secrets for making paper airplanes and will answer e-mail questions submitted to him. If you want to know, for example, whether you can catch germs from handling money, simple ask McDonald. By the way, the lower the denomination of currency, the greater the chance of catching germs.

For other information contained in this site, see Chapter 7—Music and Radio—Canadian Broadcasting Corporation.

Look, Learn, and Do

http://www.looklearnanddo.com/documents/home.html

The authors of *Look, Learn, and Do* books will teach your students how to build blimps, bug nets, windmills, compasses, greenhouses, and sailboats from everyday items such as milk cartons and straws. The projects are easy and the directions clear. Each object includes a history and brief scientific explanations as well as a list of resources for those interested in further research. The authors should be commended on the lack of commercialism at the site.

Miami Museum of Science

http://www.miamisci.org

The Science Learning Network at the Miami Museum of Science offers a fun activity- and inquiry-based field trip, where your students can learn about atoms and molecules, various kinds and forms of energy, pH factors, weather and natural disasters, and how to use the Internet for inquiry-based learning. To find these exhibits, follow the museum map to education and then to online education resources / SLN. The *Atoms Family* exhibit is an example of the types of activities your students will be able to participate in. Students can help the Mummy build a better-insulated pyramid, show Dracula how to reflect light and create shadows and afterimages of bats, click on several gases and different places on a thermometer to watch animations of how the molecules and compositions of the elements change from liquid to gas to solids, and build a roller coaster to entertain the monster family by using the concepts of kinetic and potential energy. The *pH Gallery* offers complete teachers' guides and units. Lesson plans include materials lists (almost all of which are everyday, readily available items), activities, explanatory texts, and a choice of postunit assessments, including performance, authentic/project, portfolio, and journal assessments. Teachers who are unsure about navigating the Internet and how to use it for inquiry-based learning will want to visit *Internet Island.*

Museum of Science and Industry

http://www.msichicago.org/info/infohome.html

Chicago's Museum of Science and Industry is the oldest museum of its kind in the Western hemisphere and the first to develop hands-on exhibits. Be sure to take your students to the CB&O Railroad to watch the development of the famous Pioneer Zephyr. They will learn how this train works and how it was designed, using an efficient diesel electric engine, streamlining the body, lowering the train's center of gravity, and using stainless steel for construction. Younger students will not want to miss Colleen Moore's enchanted fairy castle. Be sure to tell your students to duck their heads while wandering through the castle—it's scaled at 1 inch for every foot. The furniture and walls are filled with precious gems and gold as well as original works of art by many of the twentieth century's most famous writers, composers, and artists. The princess's bedroom, for example, has platinum chairs set with diamonds, and the backs of the chairs are emerald and diamond clips. Other exhibits include hatching chicks and a simulated tour of the doomed Flight 727, complete with an explanation of the "black box."

For other information contained in this site, see Chapter 8—Mining and Natural Resource Management—Museum of Science and Industry.

Oregon Museum of Science

http://www.omsi.edu

There's something of interest for students of all ages at the Oregon Museum of Science, including a tour of a Pacific Northwest forest, the recipe for "flubber," and an exhibit on the engineering and science of fountains (older students will learn how to build their own fountains). The forest tour, geared toward grades 3–8, allows students to step into a time machine to see the origin of a forest and follow its cycle into the future. They will learn why shade-tolerant trees eventually take over while learning about forest cycles, management, products, and resources. New exhibits are constantly added, and it's not always clear from the initial descriptions whether you will find a genuine online activity or mere photographs of actual museum exhibits. To save time, stick with the *Chem Lab* and the clearly designated *Online Activities*.

Science Museum of Minnesota

http://www.sci.mus.mn.us

Does mold grow faster on fresh bread or day-old toast? Stop by the *Thinking Fountain* at the Science Museum of Minnesota to find the answer. They will even show you how to grow your own molds, and they will post the most interesting results on-site. If molds aren't your cup of tea, there are plenty of other ideas indexed alphabetically by topic. Just about any field of science is covered. If you don't want to be cooped up in a laboratory, join one of the outside field trips, such as a visit to Vollis Simpson's whirligig farm in North Carolina, where you can learn to design a pneumatic machine. Or, go further to Catalhoyuk and join an international team busy excavating this ancient Turkish city. They will let you choose a burial site to uncover and will answer all of your questions, such as why the teeth of these ancient people had no cavities. The team will even engage your students in ethical debates, such as whether or not it is right for scientists to study human remains.

INVENTIONS

See also Chapter 12—Edison, Thomas Alva, *and* Goldberg, Reuben Lucius (Rube).

Alexander Graham Bell's Path to the Telephone

http://jefferson.village.virginia.edu/albell/homepage.html

When Alexander Graham Bell began his experiments, he wasn't thinking about a telephone but about the cutting-edge technology of the day—the multiple telegraph. Through a series of flowcharts that include Bell's original sketches and writings from his notebooks, experiments, patents, court depositions, and correspondence, the path to his ultimate invention is traced. Students are able to follow the scientific process and delve into the mind, motivations, and hurdles faced by this famous inventor.

Birth of the Radio

http://www.alpcom.it/hamradio

Long-distance communication started with Darius I (552–486 B.C.E.), who sent messages from his capital to the provinces through a line of shouting men positioned on various heights. Messages transmitted in this manner traveled 30 times faster than those sent by courier. This site traces early communication from Darius to Guglielmo Marconi's invention of the radio just over 100 years ago. There is biographical information, photographs, and even Marconi's voice (in Italian). This self-taught man, more interested in practice than scientific theories, disproved the common belief of scientists that electromagnetic waves could only be transmitted in a straight line and only if nothing was in the way. Marconi created such a political stir that he was unable to pursue development of his invention in his native Italy and had to go to England for funding and support. There are also photographic reviews of old radios and of Marconi and his experiments and images of faxes sent from his daughter and grandchild to administrators of the site.

Innovation Network

http://innovate.si.edu/welcome.html

The Computerworld Smithsonian Awards Program was established in 1989 to document the progress of the information technology revolution. Each year, awards are given in the areas of leadership, innovators, global integration, breakthrough science, and education. Current and previous award winners such as Seymour Cray and Robert Ballard (developer of the Jason project) are presented at this site. Students are able to read brief biographies of each award winner and gain some insight into their inventions and how they have changed the world. There are also oral and video histories of such notables as Bill Gates, Steve Jobs, and Anne Meyer, who pioneered the use of computers for the learning disabled. Previous award winners include Jay Forrester (who developed core memory for computers),

Robert Metcalfe (developer of the Ethernet), Vinton Cerf (the "father of the Internet"), and William Hewlett and David Packard (before establishing Hewlett-Packard, they supplied the audio oscillators for Walt Disney's *Fantasia*).

Inventure Place

http://www.invent.org/inventure.html

Inventure Place, the site of the National Inventors Hall of Fame in Akron, Ohio, has short biographies and audio clips of inventors inducted into the institution. In addition to the old standbys like Thomas Edison and Alexander Graham Bell, your students can meet such people as Ernst Alexanderson, the General Electric engineer whose high-frequency alternator gave the United States its start in the field of radio communication. (He was also the first to transmit a facsimile message across the Atlantic.) Other inductees include Luis Walter Alvarez, a Nobel Prize winner in the field of physics, and Edwin Howard Armstrong, whose crowning achievement was the development of the FM radio. Students who have an interest in inventing will want to learn about the various summer camps and programs sponsored by the National Inventors Hall of Fame.

Unusual Inventions

http://colitz.com

Did you ever want to give yourself a pat on the back or change the shape of your nose? Patent attorney Michael J. Colitz shares unusual inventions that have received U.S. patents. The actual sketches and descriptions submitted to the Patent Office are shown, so you not only see the invention and how it works but also understand the reasoning of the inventor. For example, Ralph Piro says his "pat on the back apparatus" is "useful for amusement or a needed psychological lift." We suppose the eye shade for chickens serves a similarly useful purpose. For those who think they may have a better idea than those presented at the site, Colitz provides an overview of the patent process.

PALEONTOLOGY

http://www.mwc.mus.co.us/dinosaurs/index.htm

The dinosaur collection at the Museum of Western Colorado in Grand Junction is so impressive that the U.S. Post Service issued commemorative stamps depicting some of the museum's "residents." Curators will take you through the laboratories and back rooms, where you can learn how fossils and bones are prepared for study and exhibition. Or, wander through the various exhibits and view skeletons, robotic dinosaurs, and fossilized skin.

PHYSICS

The Frog That Learned to Fly

http://www-hfml.sci.kun.nl/hfml/levitate.html

Physicists at the High Field Magnet Laboratory at the University of Nijmegen, in Amsterdam, have levitated a frog, and they've got photographs, movies, and a scientific explanation to prove it. In fact, they believe that it's possible to magnetically levitate every natural and living creature on Earth. They will explain the concept in both simple and complex terms.

Life, Universe, and the Electron

http://www.iop.org/Physics/Electron/Exhibition

Has it already been 100 years since the electron was discovered? Visit the Science Museum of London and the Institute of Physics to view the theories and experiments leading to J. J. Thomson's 1897 discovery of electrons. Thomson talks about his discovery, and administrators provide an animation of his original experiment. We've come a long way since the 1940 cavity magnetron (which led to the invention of microwave ovens). Now, our knowledge of electrons has enabled us to construct the Hubble telescope, and your students can see photos taken with it. They will also learn other ways in which electrons are used in our daily lives and how they help us understand the creation and content of the universe.

The Particle Adventure

http://pdg.lbl.gov/cpep/adventure.html

Come to the Lawrence Berkeley National Laboratory to explore the inner workings of the atom through this introduction to the theory of fundamental particles (the Standard Model) and forces. Teachers may want to visit this site first—there are free supplementary materials to order from the Contemporary Physics Education Project, a nonprofit organization of physicists, teachers, and educators. These materials accompany a seven-lesson unit on particle theory and its applications, geared toward middle and upper-level students. However, students at all levels will still enjoy other parts of the tour, which include movies, other classroom activities, quizzes, a glossary, and a pronunciation guide. Information is also available in Spanish, Polish, and French.

Physics Exhibits

http://scitech.mus.il.us

Students can learn about atoms, quarks, and gluons courtesy of SciTech, a hands-on science center in Aurora, Illinois. There they can manipulate a working model of a hydrogen atom to see the principles of uncertainty in action. Cartoon figures illustrate and explain the six quarks currently known to physicists and show students how to create their own particles. A second tour, sponsored by the Illinois State Board of Education and developed by SciTech with help from scientists at Fermilab and the John G. Shedd Aquarium, covers the physics of aquatic animals and their environments. Geared toward grades 4–6, this interactive exhibit integrates biology, geography, oceanography, and math, with the primary focus on the exploration of the principles of density and pressure, the velocity of sound, the bending of light, and electrical conductivity. For example, students will learn how a shark uses the electrical conductivity of water to navigate long distances using the Earth's magnetic field and the Farady Effect. They will also be able to see through the eyes of a barracuda, use a swim bladder, and echolocate like a dolphin.

Twentieth-Century Physics

http://www.colorado.edu/physics/2000

Faculty from the University of Colorado will take your students on an interactive journey through modern physics and its applications to devices used in everyday life. The journey helps students of all ages explore how Albert Einstein's theories led to such inventions as X-rays, lasers, and microwave ovens. Students are even able to perform X-rays of a human hand. Others might prefer to visit the atomic lab, where they can participate in twentieth-century atomic physics experiments.

TECHNOLOGY

See also Chapter 6—Mobiles and Kinetic Sculptures.

Xavier the Robot

http://www.cs.cmu.edu/~Xavier/lab.html

Xavier the Robot resides at the Learning Robot Lab at Carnegie Mellon University's (CMU) Robotics Institute. Professors and students at the School of Computer Science are focusing on the development of a robot with perceptual reasoning that will operate in an office environment for long periods of time while continuously improving performance through learning. It doesn't sound much different from what you are trying to accomplish with your students, and perhaps you will get more cooperation by letting them visit this site and operate Xavier. They are able to tell him which room to go to, say "hi," take a photograph, or tell a knock-knock joke. He'll even send e-mail to your students. There is a background on Xavier's development and how he works. At the current time, CMU is working on Amelia, an improvement on Xavier.

CHAPTER 11

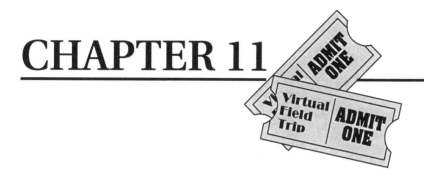

HEALTH, SAFETY, AND FITNESS

Private industry, the federal government, and concerned professionals have all opened their doors to virtual field trips to teach your students about safety, nutrition, and physical fitness. We're especially pleased to present two field trips that encourage students of different physical capabilities and ethnicities to understand each other: the Justice Department and Band Aids and Blackboards, a labor of love from a professor of nursing. Of course, it's easier to enjoy your friends if you are not convalescing from roller-skating, bicycling, automobile, or sports accidents; suffering from decaying teeth; or using drugs, alcohol, or tobacco. We've found lots of straight paths that take off into the farthest reaches of cyberspace—from Washington, DC, to the world of clowns. Be sure to stop at the Nutrition Café for lunch.

BAND AIDS AND BLACKBOARDS
http://funrsc.fairfield.edu/~jfleitas/contents.html

Joan Fleitas, assistant professor of nursing at Connecticut's Fairfield University, wants to teach children what it is like to grow up with severe or chronic physical or mental conditions. There are separate sections for younger students, teenagers, and adults, where the disabled children, their siblings, and parents share their stories, perspectives, and photographs. Fleitas discusses the usual taunts, insults, and unconscious reactions to the children, and she also lists actual retorts and strategies children have used to maintain their dignity. She reassures both the disabled children and their classmates, reminding everyone that conditions are not contagious and that asking them about their conditions shows that you care. All students, she says, should focus on what they can rather than cannot do, and she points out how boring the world would be if we were all the same ("How would you know where you stop and another person begins?").

BASKETBALL HALL OF FAME
http://www.hooptown.com

Pay a visit to the Basketball Hall of Fame in Springfield, Massachusetts, the birthplace of the game. The institution honors players from high school and college as well as from professional leagues. Your tour begins at *Hoops BC* (before the clock), with a history of the game and its inventor, Dr. James Naismith. Students will learn how the shot clock revolutionized the sport in the 1950s. *The Pros* includes a collection of memorabilia and trophies as well as biographies of some of the world's greatest players. However, the Hall of Fame places more emphasis on high school and college basketball. Older students will want to visit *High School Hoops,* which examines the origins of high school basketball and its impact on some of the game's greatest players. Check the latest National Basketball Association news, which is updated every minute.

BENNY GOODSPORT
http://www.bennygoodsport.com

Benny Goodsport the clown and his gang will teach your students all about physical fitness and nutrition through simple activities, games, stories, and cartoons. The nice thing about Benny is that he's happy to get e-mail from children and ready to listen and respond to all of their problems, questions, and comments. Nine-year-old Desean Garnett wrote, "Sports can be dangerous because I was playing baseball one time and I wasn't paying attentoin to the game and got wacked with the baseball right in the eye." Benny agreed that sports can be dangerous, so it's important to wear protective clothing. Other children just write, "Dear Benny—You ROCK!!" Benny and the gang also realize that everyone isn't an athlete, so they give as much attention to fishing and walking as to kickball and soccer. Children are encouraged to play the food pyramid game and submit their own healthy menus, many of which are posted at the site. By the way, Benny is really Sondra Arbeter Webber, a computer programmer.

CALIFORNIA STATE AUTOMOBILE ASSOCIATION
http://www.ottoclub.org

Otto the automobile will teach your children how to stay safe—while playing, riding in a car, biking, and skating, and as a pedestrian. This is all done through pictures and games. There are safety posters drawn by children, and games such as the *Dressing Room,* where you choose a friend to dress appropriately for various kinds of weather.

DEPARTMENT OF JUSTICE
http://www.usdoj.gov/kidspage

Your students will learn all about health, safety, and crime prevention from the Department of Justice. There are two tours—one for grades K–5 and one for grades 6–12. There is a discussion about Internet safety for younger students, but the primary portion of the tour deals with conflict resolution. Students will read short stories about children of different races, religions, and cultures who face prejudice and problems in the playground, lunchroom, classroom, and neighborhood. They are then asked to choose a solution. For example, when classmates tell a young Asian student that she can't play the role of Snow White, your students decide whether the child should accept this decision, talk to an adult, or ask the students to explain why someone must look exactly like a person in a book. Older students can read a multimedia book about drugs and learn how to get involved in crime prevention. The book, accompanied by suggested classroom activities, can easily be adapted for an entire drug prevention unit. The Federal Bureau of Investigation (FBI) will share information about civil rights, DNA testing, fingerprint imprints, forensic science, polymer testing, U.S. marshals, and the role of the federal prosecutor. Teachers may want to check the site first because some of the materials include details about the FBI's ten most wanted criminals as well as some rather unsavory famous cases.

DR. RABBIT'S NO CAVITIES CLUBHOUSE
http://www.colgate.com/Kids-world/index.html

Dr. Rabbit, who works for Colgate, will teach your students all about oral hygiene in the privacy of their very own clubhouse. He'll even introduce children to his personal friend, the tooth fairy (even the tooth fairy has gone high tech—she'll communicate with your students via e-mail). There are lots of things to do in the clubhouse: learning healthy habits through connect-the-dots, coloring, searching the jungle for healthy foods, and saving a tooth from the plaque monster. Check the monthly winners of the "My Bright Smile Global Poster Contest"—they will share their artwork with you and tell you about their hometowns.

FDA KID'S PAGE
http://www.fda.gov/oc/opacom/kids/default.htm

The Food and Drug Administration (FDA) would like to introduce your students to Yorick the bionic skeleton, who's loaded with electronic devices and mechanical parts and synthetic replacement body parts. Click on any part of his body, such as his silicone ear implant, glass eye, pacemaker, artificial joints, or bone growth stimulator to learn about these medical devices and how they work. Other parts of the site deal with safe food handling, pets, vaccines, and tobacco. There's a special section for teenagers, which deals with such pertinent topics as acne, cosmetics, dieting, and smoking.

INDIAN HEALTH SERVICE
http://www.ihs.gov/publicinfo/publications/mcgruff1/parents.asp

Follow the *Adventures of McGruff and Scruff in Indian Country*, courtesy of the Indian Health Service and the Federal Bureau of Justice Assistance. Although Scruff has learned a lot about drug, alcohol, gangs, weapons, and violence prevention from his Uncle McGruff, he still gets himself into the kinds of sticky situations that many children are likely to encounter, and sometimes your students will have to help him decide what to do. As in real life, every choice has its consequences. For example, Johnny takes his father's gun out of the closet and shows it to Scruff, assuring him that it's not loaded. Students must decide whether Scruff should tell Johnny to put the gun back, go home and talk to an adult, or be "cool" and play with the gun. They can also play the *What If* game, a multiple choice quiz in which students must decide what to do if someone asks them to drink, they encounter a bully, or they face domestic abuse. Although materials are presented in a comic book format, teachers should be cautioned that rather sophisticated topics such as sniffing chemicals are presented.

NATIONAL CRIME PREVENTION COUNCIL
http://www.ncpc.org/child.htm

The National Crime Prevention Council wants your students to be safe, and in this effort, this tour covers the gamut of topics from back-to-school safety tips and bicycle helmets to date rape. Fortunately, separate tours have been arranged for ages 5–12, ages 13–21, and adults who work with both age groups. Games and activities for younger students include crossword puzzles, word scrambles, connect-the-dots, and the *Silly and Dangerous Game,* in which children decide which items in a picture are silly and which are dangerous. Older students can test their street IQ or learn how to recognize whether one of their friends is taking drugs and what to do about it. Information is also provided about topics such as vandalism, alcohol abuse, violence prevention, and baby-sitting.

NATIONAL HIGHWAY TRAFFIC SAFETY ADMINISTRATION
http://www.nhtsa.dot.gov/kids

Vince and Larry, the crash test dummies, will guide your students through *Safety City,* where they will learn all about current safety events, bicycle helmets, seatbelts, and other safety issues. They will introduce your students to Garrett A. Morgan, who invented the traffic safety signal, take them to the theater where such movies as Ray Charles's musical *Back Seat Baby* are playing, and guide them safely through Safety City by bike or foot. Teachers can relax in the lounge and order some free materials. Your students will be safe with Vince and Larry, who have been the victims of many crashes and will, as a result, ensure that your students participate in safe equipment checks, wear the proper clothing, and watch for the particular dangers of city biking. They will also tell them about the safety features of school buses and take them on a tour of the research lab, which includes the crash test grounds, the seatbelt room, the carseat area, the airbag room, and warnings about drinking and drugs.

NATIONAL INSTITUTE ON DRUG ABUSE
http://165.112.78.61/MOM/MOMIndex.html

Students in grades 5–9 are invited to join Sarah Bellum on her *Mind Over Matter* tour of the human brain and body and learn how they are affected by drugs. The tour, produced by the National Institute on Drug Abuse, National Institutes of Health, is a series of six magazines, each of which is devoted to a specific drug or drug group, including marijuana, opiates, inhalants, hallucinogens, nicotine, stimulants, and steroids. A teacher's guide is provided, which contains objectives, background information, and classroom activities.

NUTRITION CAFÉ
http://exhibits.pacsci.org/nutrition

Are you looking for an alternative to the fast food restaurants often frequented by students? Try the *Nutrition Café,* operated by the Pacific Science Center and the Washington State Dairy Council. If you are not sure what to order, owners will help you plan a nutritious meal at the *Have a Bite Café.* Or, play some of the games. Detective Inspector Snarfengood needs some help finding the missing nutrient in this site's version of *Hangman.* Or try your hand at *Card a Grape,* a version of *Jeopardy.* The tour also includes a glossary and an interactive food pyramid.

CHAPTER 12

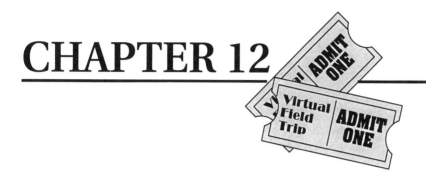

PEOPLE YOU SHOULD KNOW

You've heard a lot about how the Internet—for better or for worse—is an easy way to meet people. We've assembled an international cast of people from your students' favorite authors to historical figures—not just the movers and shakers but ordinary people who have done extraordinary acts of community and public service. Oh, and say "hi" to Galileo for us. We'd go along, but we promised Buffalo Bill that we'd go on a hunt with him.

ALCOTT, LOUISA MAY
http://www.louisamayalcott.org/alcottorchard.html

This is a tour of the home where Louisa May Alcott lived from 1858 to 1877 and what is generally believed to be the setting for *Little Women*. Highlights include the dining room where conversations about abolitionism, women's suffrage, and social reform were held; her bedroom where she wrote; and biographies of her father, Amos Bronson Alcott, who was a transcendental philosopher and teacher, and her mother, Abagail May—one of the first paid social workers in Massachusetts.

ALTGELD, JOHN PETER
See Chapter 3—United States—Illinois—Chicago's Graveyards.

ANTHONY, SUSAN B.
See Chapter 1—Women's History—National Register of Historic Places.

ANTOINETTE, MARIE

See Chapter 1—French History—Chateau de Versailles.

ARMSTRONG, LOUIS

See Chapter 3—United States—Louisiana—New Orleans.

ARMSTRONG, NEIL

See Chapter 1—Military History—United States Air Force.

ASK AN EXPERT

http://www.askanexpert.com/askanexpert/cat

Imagine having access to hundreds of experts throughout the world! Pittsco, an educational technology company, has compiled a list of more than 300 experts in virtually every field who are willing to answer questions via e-mail. The list is topically organized by science and technology, careers and industry, health, the Internet and computers, recreation and entertainment, education and personal development, intercultural, money, fine arts, and religion. Administrators ask that you first check the archives for responses to previously asked questions before submitting a request. Ask about President Abraham Lincoln, college admission requirements, math, manners, English as a second language, and just about anything else you want to know. Because the experts come from various organizations and companies, their motivations for volunteering their time are occasionally commercial or ideological. However, all affiliations are clearly identified, and Pittsco shows you where to go on the Internet to find additional information about the experts. We suggest you check each expert's affiliations before permitting students to e-mail them.

BABBAGE, CHARLES

See Chapter 9—Mathematicians.

BACON, HENRY

See Chapter 3—United States—Washington, D.C.—Lincoln Memorial.

BALLARD, ROBERT

See Chapter 10—Inventions—Innovation Network.

BARTON, CLARA

See Chapter 1—Military History—Civil War Tour 3.

BECHET, SIDNEY

See Chapter 3—United States—Louisiana—New Orleans.

BELL, ALEXANDER GRAHAM

See Chapter 1—U.S. History—PBS American Experience Series *and* Chapter 10—Inventions—Alexander Graham Bell's Path to the Telephone.

BERG, MORRIS (MOE)

See Chapter 3—United States—Central Intelligence Agency.

BERING, VITUS

See Chapter 1—Maritime History—Maritime Museum of British Columbia.

BERRY, MARTHA

See Chapter 1—U.S. History—Georgia.

BINI, DANTE

See Chapter 2—Alternative Architecture—Bini's Concrete Structures.

BLUME, JUDY

http://www.judyblume.com/home-menu.html

Did you ever wonder how authors get ideas for stories, or if they have a favorite story book character? Author Judy Blume will be happy to answer any questions your students might have. (By the way, she treats her characters like her own children, so of course she does not play favorites.) Blume will share writing tips with your students and her views on such topics as censorship. She feels that censorship is a result of fear and that "It's not just the books under fire now that worry me. It is the books that will never be written. The books that will never be read."

BLY, NELLIE

See Chapter 1—U.S. History—PBS American Experience Series.

BOONE, DANIEL

See Chapter 1—U.S. History—American West Tour.

BOWIE, JAMES

See Chapter 1—U.S. History—American West Tour.

BRETT, JAN

http://www.janbrett.com

Younger students will enjoy visiting with Jan Brett, author of such children's novels as *The Hat*, *Comet's Nine Lives*, and *Berlioz the Bear*. Brett will tell you a bit about herself, and you can actually hear her speak. She provides many activities in conjunction with her works, such as coloring pages, recipes for Annie's Corn Cakes (the same ones that appear in *Annie and the Wild Animals*), and crafts. She'll even show you how she draws some of her illustrations. Brett welcomes e-mail from her fans.

BRYANT, GRIDLEY J. F.

See Chapter 2—American Architecture—Tour 2.

BULFINCH, CHARLES

See Chapter 2—American Architecture—Tour 2.

BURNHAM, DANIEL

See Chapter 3—United States—Illinois—Chicago's Graveyards.

CABRILLO, JUAN

See Chapter 3—United States—California—Cabrillo National Monument.

CALAMITY JANE

See Chapter 1—American West—Colorado Lore, Legend, and Fact.

CAPOTE, TRUMAN

See Chapter 3—United States—Louisiana—New Orleans.

CARNEGIE, ANDREW

See Chapter 1—U.S. History—PBS American Experience Series.

CARSON, CHRISTOPHER HOUSTON (KIT)

See Chapter 1—U.S. History—American West Tour.

CASSIDY, BUTCH

See Chapter 1—U.S. History—American West—Colorado Lore, Legend, and Fact.

CATT, CARRIE CHAPMAN

See Chapter 1—Women's History—Women in History.

CAUCHY, AUGUSTIN LOUIS

See Chapter 9—Mathematicians.

CERF, VINTON

See Chapter 10—Inventions—Innovation Network.

CERMAK, ANTON

See Chapter 3—United States—Illinois—Chicago's Graveyards.

CLARK, WILLIAM

See Chapter 1—U.S. History—Lewis and Clark Expedition.

CLEBURNE, PATRICK

See Chapter 1—U.S. History—Georgia.

CLINTON, HILLARY RODHAM

See Chapter 1—Women's History—Women in History.

COCHRAN, JACQUELINE

See Chapter 1—Military History—World War II—Women's Air Force Service Pilots.

CODY, WILLIAM FREDERICK (BUFFALO BILL)
http://www.AmericanWest.com

By the time he was 22 years old, Buffalo Bill had been a trapper, a bullwhacker, a Colorado Fifty-Niner, a Pony Express Rider, a wagon master, a stagecoach driver, a Civil War soldier, and a hotel manager. He became a scout for the U.S. Army in 1868 and stayed until 1872—a record for this particular profession. With all of these experiences, he has a lot of interesting thoughts to share with your students. His views on the political climate of the time are most interesting: "Every Indian outbreak I have ever known has resulted from broken promises and broken treaties from the go." He was one of the original environmentalists and women's advocates. During a 1894 newspaper interview, he shared his thoughts on some of these matters. When asked if the majority of women were qualified to vote, he responded: "As well qualified as the majority of men." As for equal rights, he stated: "If a woman can do the same work that a man can do and do it just as well she should have the same pay." Your students can visit with Buffalo Bill and other Western notables such as James Bowie, Davy Crockett, Daniel Boone (more than any other man, he was responsible for the exploration and settlement of Kentucky), and Christopher Houston (Kit) Carson ("his word was as sure as the sun comin' up"), by following the path *Famous Pioneers and Frontiersmen*.

See also Chapter 1—U.S. History—American West Tour.

COLUMBUS, CHRISTOPHER

See Chapter 1—1492.

COOK, CAPTAIN JAMES

See Chapter 1—Maritime History—Maritime Museum of British Columbia.

CORNET, ANTONI GAUDI

See Chapter 2—Gaudi, Antoni.

COUSTEAU, JACQUES

http://www.weburbia.com/pg/cousteau.htm

"When I dive, I feel like an angel," said Jacques Cousteau, possibly the most famous oceanographer and environmental activist of the twentieth century. Take your students to pay an homage to the man, his works, and his famous ships, *Calypso* and *Calypso II*. Hear tributes, many of them poetic, from around the world, in English and French. Your students can also hear the National Public Radio and CNN tributes to Cousteau. Students who want to practice their French can also go to the Cousteau Society to learn more about the man at **www.cousteau.org**.

CRAY, SEYMOUR

See Chapter 10—Inventions—Innovation Network.

CROCKETT, DAVY

See Chapter 1—U.S. History—American West Tour.

DE GAULLE, CHARLES

See Chapter 1—French History—Chateau de Versailles.

DE PAOLA, TOMIE

See Chapter 3—United States—New York—Greece Central School District.

DESOTO, HERNANDO

See Chapter 1—U.S. History—Georgia.

DOMINO, ANTOINE (FATS)

See Chapter 3—United States—Louisiana—New Orleans.

DONOVAN, WILLIAM

See Chapter 3—United States—Central Intelligence Agency.

DOUGLASS, FREDERICK

See Chapter 3—United States—Maryland.

DRAKE, FRANCIS

See Chapter 1—Maritime History—Maritime Museum of British Columbia.

EARHART, AMELIA

See also Chapter 10—Aviation and Aerospace—Flight.
http://www.ionet.net/~jellenc/ae_intro.html

This site provides a detailed life history of the famous aviatrix from birth to the celebrity years through the final flight. Amelia Earhart's life changed forever when she received a telephone call from Captain H. H. Railey, who inquired: "How would you like to be the first woman to fly across the Atlantic?" Although Earhart was merely a passenger on this highly publicized flight, the fame she received allowed her to schedule increasingly risky flights around the world. Upon leaving for the last flight, she said: "I have a feeling that there is just one more good flight left in my system and I hope this trip is it." Neither Earhart nor her plane was ever found after this fateful flight, but there are lessons she would have wanted us to have learned from her experience: "Please know that I am quite aware of the hazards. . . . Women must try to do things as men have tried. When they fail, their failure must be a challenge to others."

EARP, WYATT

See Chapter 1—U.S. History—American West—Colorado—Lore, Legend, and Fact.

EDISON, THOMAS ALVA
http://www.nps.gov/htdocs2/edis/homepg.htm

The National Park Service will introduce you to Thomas Edison, or "Al" as his friends and family knew him. By the way, if you ask Edison whether he is in fact a genius, he'll tell you that "genius is hard work, stick-to-it-iveness, and common sense." Edison was home-schooled because he was such a poor student, although he loved to read and do experiments in the basement. His very first invention, the electric vote recorder, was a failure. Although he said, "I have not heard a bird sing since I was 12," he invented the phonograph. The site profiles this invention as well as the electric lightbulb and motion pictures.

EINSTEIN, ALBERT
http://www.westegg.com/einstein/

"My intellectual development was retarded; as a result I began to wonder about space and time only when I had already grown up," says Albert Einstein. Don't let this happen to *your* students. Aside from being one of the most quotable scientists in the world, Einstein's legacy is so profound that we can probably only begin to understand it. Here's a good place to start that exploration. There are at least ten separate biographical sketches of Einstein here, so you are sure to find one for your class's level. There are also dozens of photographs, from the classics to such incongruous ones as Einstein in downtown Pittsburgh. Students will be amused and fascinated by his quotes, which are organized by topic. Before your class leaves, be sure to join people all around the world in signing the birthday cybercard to Einstein.

ELMSLIE, GEORGE GRANT
See Chapter 2—Prairie School of Architecture.

FERMI, ENRICO
See Chapter 3—United States—Illinois—Chicago's Graveyards.

FERRARO, GERALDINE
See Chapter 1—Women's History—Women in History.

FIELD, MARSHALL

See Chapter 3—United States—Illinois—Chicago's Graveyards.

FISHER, CARL

See Chapter 1—United States History—PBS American Experience Series.

FISHER, IRVING

See Chapter 8—Money, Banking, and Economics—Federal Reserve Bank.

FITZGERALD, F. SCOTT
http://www.sc.edu/fitzgerald/index.html

The University of South Carolina has established this comprehensive site covering the life and works of F. Scott Fitzgerald. It has been said that Fitzgerald's life overshadowed his works. Through audio and film clips, copies of his works, interviews, chronologies, essays, and articles, this site gives a balanced portrayal of the author and the dominant influences of his life—aspiration, literature, Princeton, Zelda Sayre Fitzgerald, and alcohol.

FORD, ROBERT

See Chapter 1—U.S. History—American West—Colorado—Lore, Legend, and Fact.

FORREST, NATHAN BEDFORD

See Chapter 1—U.S. History—Georgia.

FORRESTER, JAY

See Chapter 10—Inventions—Innovation Network.

FRANK, ANNE

Anne Frank Center USA
http://www.annefrank.com

Anne Frank's diary has been translated into 55 languages and is one of the most widely read books in the world. The Anne Frank Center USA will show you actual pages from Anne's diary and explain how it was authenticated and came to be published. Anne's story is told through photographs and texts. As we went to press, administrators promised that sections on the Holocaust and classroom activities would be added soon.

Anne Frank House

http://www.annefrank.nl

Take your students on a tour of the house in which Anne Frank, her mother and father, the Van Pels family, and Fritz Pfeffer spent two years cut off from the outside world. They will learn the story of Anne and see excerpts from her diary in Anne's own handwriting. Of particular interest are the often neglected, rewritten portions of the diary that Anne planned to publish as a book entitled *The Secret Annex*. Teachers will want to check the suggested classroom activities and discussion topics.

FRANKLIN, BENJAMIN

See Chapter 3—United States—Central Intelligence Agency.

FRENCH, DANIEL CHESTER

See Chapter 3—United States—Washington, D.C.—Lincoln Memorial.

FREUD, SIGMUND

http://freud.t0.or.at

Pay a visit to the Sigmund Freud Museum in Vienna and spend some time with the father of psychoanalysis. Visits with Freud and his friends, family, and associates can be conducted in either English or German. In addition to his home, you can visit his clinics and other workplaces. If he's too busy with patients, you can always spend some time with Anna Freud, who will be more than happy to share personal and professional views of her famous father. Our favorite spot on the tour was the media library, which includes amateur movies filmed between 1930 and 1939 in Paris, Vienna, and London. The majority of the films were taken by Marie Bonaparte and were meant for private purposes because Freud was rather publicity-shy. They are silent films, so if you want to hear the words of Freud himself, visit the audio library, where you can listen to his 1938 interview with the British Broadcasting Corporation.

GALILEO

http://es.rice.edu/ES/humsoc/Galileo

Rice University's *Galileo Project* is a multimedia source of information on the life and works of the man and the science and culture of his time. Students can go back in time to Galileo's villa, where each room presents a different aspect of his life and career. For example, the laboratory provides information about Galileo's inquiries into physics. Students will be able to look through Galileo's telescope and recreate the actual scientific experiments that he conducted. Be sure to leave some time for tours of Florence and Tuscany, where you will learn about music, architecture, and culture. You may be lucky enough to run into Niccolò Machiavelli, Michelangelo, or the Medicis. Be sure to watch your manners—there was very specific etiquette in earlier times. During our tour, we were given the following advice: "When you are eating, do not masticate noisily or crouch gluttonously over the food without raising your face, as if you were blowing a trumpet. Avoid rubbing your teeth with your napkin, or worse yet still with your fingers. Do not scratch yourself, or spit, or at least do it reservedly. After blowing your nose, do not look into your hand-kerchief as if pearls or rubies had been deposited into it and refrain from long descriptions of your dreams, as though they were interesting."

GATES, BILL

See Chapter 10—Inventions—Innovation Network.

GAUDI, ANTONI

See Chapter 2—Gaudi, Antoni.

GAUSS, CARL FRIEDRICH

See Chapter 9—Mathematicians.

GIRAFFE PROJECT
http://www.giraffe.org/

How about taking your students to meet some decent role models—students and adults who initiate projects to make the world a better place? They can meet the class that raised funds in their own community to build a school playground in a Third World country, or the inner-city students who took it upon themselves to chase out drug dealers and clean garbage and litter off their streets. The nonprofit Giraffe Project provides inspirational stories, curriculum guides for K–12 teachers, and a chance for students to nominate their own giraffes—people who stick their neck out to make things better.

GODDARD, ROBERT

See Chapter 2—Military History—United States Air Force.

GOLDBERG, REUBEN LUCIUS (RUBE)
http://www.rube-goldberg.com

So you think your high school's floor plan is confusing? Take a look at some of the inventions of Reuben Lucius Goldberg, the Pulitzer Prize–winning cartoonist, sculptor, and engineer, known for his inventions that used maximum effort to gain minimal results. Several of Goldberg's inventions are described in all their loony details, including the automatic pencil sharpener and the alarm clock in which a magnifying glass burns a hole in a paper bag that drops water into a ladle that lifts a gate, allowing a ball to roll into a chute, which lifts a bed that drops its occupant into a pair of shoes. Rube thought of everything. You can't even get back into bed because it remains upright. We're told that his inventions actually worked! Those who are interested can enter the annual Rube Goldberg contest.

GRANT, ULYSSES S.
http://www.mscomm.com/~ulysses/page152.html

Candace Scott, a high school teacher and lifelong Grant admirer, will share her extensive knowledge with your class. Just about anything you might want to know about Ulysses S. Grant, including stories about his ancestors and descendants, childhood, family, and military and political career, is available at this site. And you don't have to just take Scott's word for it—General William Tecumseh Sherman, President Abraham Lincoln, and other contemporaries and modern historians also have some things to say. You can even show your class some of the paintings that Grant did. Determined to counterbalance Grant's reputation for drinking, corruption, and political naïveté, this site presents Grant much more positively than many history books.

GREENHOW, ROSE O'NEAL

See Chapter 1—Military History—Civil War Tour 3.

GROPIUS, WALTER

See Chapter 2—Bauhaus School of Architecture.

GUERIN, JULES

See Chapter 3—United States—Washington, D.C.—Lincoln Memorial.

GUTHRIE, JANET
See Chapter 1—Women's History.

GWINNETT, BUTTON
See Chapter 1—U.S. History—Georgia.

HEANEY, SEAMUS
See Chapter 7—Language Arts and Literature—Internet Poetry Archive.

HEARST, WILLIAM RANDOLPH
See Chapter 1—U.S. History—PBS American Experience Series.

HENDRIX, JIMI
See Chapter 7—Music and Radio—Experience Music Project.

HEWLETT, WILLIAM
See Chapter 10—Inventions—Innovation Network.

HILL, VIRGINIA
See Chapter 3—United States—Central Intelligence Agency.

HOLABIRD AND ROOT
See Chapter 2—American Architecture—Tour 2.

HOLLIDAY, DOC
See Chapter 1—U.S. History—American West—Colorado—Lore, Legend, and Fact.

JAMES, JESSE
See Chapter 1—U.S. History—American West—James-Younger Gang.

JANUS, ALLEN

See Chapter 6—Photography—Janus Museum of Photography.

JEFFERSON, THOMAS

See Chapter 2—American Architecture—Tour 2.

JOBS, STEVE

See Chapter 10—Inventions—Innovation Network.

JONES, QUINCY

See Chapter 7—Music and Radio—Q Radio.

KAHLO, FRIDA

See Chapter 6—Art Museums—Frida Kahlo.

KING, JR., MARTIN LUTHER

See Chapter 3—United States—Maryland.

KLEE, PAUL

See Chapter 2—Bauhaus School of Architecture.

LA SALLE, RENE

See Chapter 1—Maritime History—Tour of the Belle.

LAFAYETTE, JAMES ARMISTEAD

See Chapter 3—United States—Central Intelligence Agency.

LAFITTE, JEAN

See Chapter 3—United States—Louisiana—New Orleans.

LATROBE, BENJAMIN HENRY

See Chapter 2—American Architecture—Tour 2.

LAWRENCE, T. E.

http://www.castle-hill-press.com/tefile/home.htm

Take your students to meet the real Lawrence of Arabia, whose life was every bit as adventurous and puzzling as the movie. Students who have seen the film can see the last photograph of Lawrence, seated jauntily on his motorcycle—the scene which begins the David Lean film. Although a serious research site, the facts of Lawrence's life are presented in clear language, and the dozens of photographs, which follow Lawrence from England to Arabia and points in between, may be the most extensive collection assembled.

LEVINE, PHILIP

See Chapter 7—Language Arts and Literature—Internet Poetry Archive.

LEWIS, C. S.

http://cslewis.drzeus.net

Pay a visit to C. S. Lewis in his study and then take your class through the wardrobe closet and into Narnia, where they will find dozens of photographs of Lewis and his surroundings, and summaries of each of the *Chronicles* and of Lewis' other fiction and nonfiction works. Aslan still hasn't lost his roar, and Narnia still has its universal, magical appeal. We suggest you also browse the guest book, where people of all ages e-mail their own memories and thoughts about the *Chronicles of Narnia.* Your class can also sign the guest book and even send a photo.

LEWIS, MERIWETHER

See Chapter 1—U.S. History—Lewis and Clark Expedition.

LINCOLN, ABRAHAM

See also Grant, Ulysses S., *and* Chapter 1—U.S. History—Nineteenth-Century Industry.

http://members.aol.com/RVSNorton/Lincoln.html

Take a trip back to 1865 with R. J. Norton, a former history teacher, to experience the assassination of President Abraham Lincoln and its aftermath. Students can delve into the mind and motivations of John Wilkes Booth and his co-conspirators, tour the Ford Theater, examine conspiracy theories, and participate in the trial. Did Booth act alone? Was the assassination a Confederate plot or the result of a conspiracy of international bankers? Check the on-site transcript of the trial proceedings and form your own conclusions. Students can also read Private John Millington's eyewitness account of the chase and capture of Booth or sit in on Lincoln's autopsy. Norton will be happy to answer any of your questions via e-mail.

LINCOLN, MARY TODD

See Chapter 1—Military History—Civil War Tour 3.

THE LONE RANGER

http://www.ticnet.com/mlargent/LR1.html

With a cloud of dust and a hearty "Hi-Yo Silver! Away!" the Lone Ranger, complete with the opening trumpets of the "William Tell Overture," rides out of the past to visit your class. Production artist Mark Largent has constructed this homage to the famous cowboy hero and his faithful Indian companion, Tonto. The site is full of little-known facts about the Lone Ranger, including his early history in movie serials, and the frequently asked questions page even reveals how the writers came up with the name Tonto. *Kemosabe*, incidentally, is an actual Pottowatomie Indian word, which means "faithful friend." We especially liked the section of quotes from the Lone Ranger, which includes gems such as, "Sooner or later, somewhere . . . somehow . . . we must settle with the world and make payment for what we have taken."

LOUIS XIV

See Chapter 1—French History—Chateau de Versailles *and* Maritime History—Tour of the Belle.

MCARTHUR, DOUGLAS

See Chapter 3—United States—California—Fort McArthur Museum.

MCKANE, JOHN

See Chapter 1—U.S. History—Coney Island.

MCKINLEY, WILLIAM

See Chapter 1—U.S. History—Nineteenth-Century Industry.

MARCONI, GUGLIELMO

See Chapter 10—Inventions—Birth of the Radio.

MARSALIS FAMILY

See Chapter 3—United States—Louisiana—New Orleans.

MASTERSON, WILLIAM

See Chapter 1—U.S. History—American West—Colorado Lore, Legend, and Fact.

METCALFE, ROBERT

See Chapter 10—Inventions—Innovation Network.

MEYER, ANNE

See Chapter 10—Inventions—Innovation Network.

MICHELANGELO

See Chapter 1—Renaissance.

MILLER, JOHN

http://www.univox.com/~barmah/jmiller

This tour covers the life and work of the "Thomas Edison of roller coasters," John A. Miller. Miller, who was responsible for the design and installation of the most famous rides in the world, was instrumental in designing safety inventions such as the friction wheel. We are told that without his inventions, there would not be any of the modern loop rides available today.

MILOSZ, CZESLAW

See Chapter 7—Language Arts and Literature—Internet Poetry Archives.

MITCHELL, BILLY

See Chapter 1—Military History—United States Air Force.

MITCHELL, MARIA

See Chapter 1—Women's History—National Register of Historic Places.

MORAN, THOMAS

http://www.ionet.net/~jellenc/moran.html

Thomas Moran, known as one of American's greatest landscape artists, produced more than 1,500 oils and 800 watercolors during his career in the nineteenth century. This site contains Moran's biography, with a focus on his paintings of Lake Superior, Yellowstone, the Grand Canyon, and the Mountain of the Holy Cross.

MORTON, FERDINAND (JELLY ROLL)

See Chapter 3—United States—Louisiana—New Orleans.

MUBARAK, HOSNEY

See Chapter 3—Egypt.

MUYBRIDGE, EADWEARD JAMES

See Chapter 6—Photography— Eadweard James Muybridge.

NAPOLEON

See Chapter 1—French History—Chateau de Versailles.

NASSY, JOSEF

See Chapter 1—Holocaust—United States Holocaust Memorial Museum.

NEWTON, ISAAC

See Chapter 9—Mathematicians.

OWENS, JESSE

See Chapter 3—United States—Illinois—Chicago's Graveyards.

PACKARD, DAVID
See Chapter 10—Inventions—Innovation Network.

PALLADIO, ANDREA
See Chapter 2—Italian Villas.

PALMER, POTTER
See Chapter 3—United States—Illinois—Chicago's Graveyards.

PASCAL, BLAISE
See Chapter 9—Mathematicians.

PAULSEN, GARY
See Chapter 3—United States—New York—Greece Central School District.

PERCY, WALKER
See Chapter 3—United States—Louisiana—New Orleans.

PINKERTON, ALLAN
See Chapter 3—United States—Illinois—Chicago's Graveyards.

PINSKY, ROBERT
See Chapter 7—Language Arts and Literature—Internet Poetry Archives.

POCAHONTAS
See Chapter 1—U.S. History—Jamestown, Virginia.

PULLMAN, GEORGE
See Chapter 3—United States—Illinois—Chicago's Graveyards.

PURCELL, WILLIAM GRAY

See Chapter 2—Prairie School of Architecture.

RICKENBACKER, EDDIE

See Chapter 1—Military History—United States Air Force.

ROGERS, WILL

http://www.ionet.net/~jellenc/rogers.html

William Penn Adair Rogers, the "Cowboy Philosopher," is known for his gentle humor, much of which is still relevant today. His charisma allowed him to deliver stinging observations and still maintain enormous popularity. "Everybody is ignorant only in different subjects," he said. This site profiles his life, from childhood, through the beginning of his professional career in 1902 as the Cherokee Kid in Texas Jack's Wild West Show in South Africa, to his fatal plane crash in Alaska.

ROLFE, JOHN

See Chapter 1—U.S. History—Jamestown, Virginia.

ROOSEVELT, THEODORE

See Chapter 1—U.S. History—PBS American Experience Series *and* Nineteenth-Century Industry.

SAINT GAUDENS, AUGUSTUS

http://www.sgnhs.org

The Saint Gaudens National Historic site in Cornish, New Hampshire, sponsors this homage to the great American sculptor. Students can pay a visit to his home and view his elaborate gardens and the local wildlife. Biographical information is accompanied by a tour of some of his greatest works, such as the Adam's Memorial in Rock Creek Cemetery and the Lincoln and General John A. Logan monuments in Chicago's Grant Park. Tours are conducted in Spanish, French, Italian, Dutch, Polish, Portuguese, and Russian.

SCHULTZ, CHARLES

http://www.unitedmedia.com/comics/peanuts

Good grief! United Media has assembled an informative collection of information on Charlie Brown and his friends, including their best friend Charles Schultz. A major asset of this site is that advertisements are clearly delineated and can be easily avoided. Your students will be interested in meeting Charles Schultz and learning that despite the fact he could receive no greater than a C+ in Section Five (Drawing of Children), he never gave up. He says: "It seem beyond the comprehension of people that someone can be born to draw comic strips, but I think I was." Schultz will introduce you to his friends Snoopy ("an extroverted beagle with a Walter Mitty Complex"), Lucy and Linus Van Pelt, Woodstock, Franklin ("the one with the fewest anxieties and obsessions"), Schroeder, Pigpen, and Marcie. Schultz is most proud of the fact that he is responsible for the introduction of the phrase "security blanket" into the English language.

SEUSS, DR.

http://www.afn.org/~afn15301/drseuss.html

"I like nonsense; it wakes up the brain cells," says Dr. Seuss, and if you are in the mood for nonsense, pay a visit to the good doctor. Did you know he didn't originally intend his books to be for children? Do you want to play the Seuss slot machine? Or would you prefer to read excerpts from his early works in the Dartmouth College humor magazine, his ads for Flit pesticides, or his short poems? You can even take the Grinch quiz, send the answers via e-mail, and see how you did. You do know where the Whos lived, don't you? There are quite a few ads at this site for Seuss-y souvenirs, so you may wish to check out your tour route ahead of time.

SHERMAN, WILLIAM T.

See Grant, Ulysses S., *and* Chapter 1—U.S. History—Georgia.

SLOCUM, JOSHUA

See Chapter 1—Maritime History—Maritime Museum of British Columbia.

SMITH, ADAM

See Chapter 8—Money, Banking, and Economics—Federal Reserve Bank.

SMITH, CAPTAIN JOHN

See Chapter 1—U.S. History—Jamestown, Virginia.

STOWE, HARRIET BEECHER

See Chapter 1—Military History—Civil War Tour 3.

SULLIVAN, LOUIS

See Chapter 2—Prairie School of Architecture *and* Chapter 3—United States—Illinois—Chicago's Graveyards.

THOMPSON, WILLIAM HALE

See Chapter 3—United States—Illinois—Chicago's Graveyards.

TUBMAN, HARRIET

See Chapter 3—United States—Maryland *and* United States—New York—Pocantico Hills School—Sleepy Hollow, New York.

TWENTIETH CENTURY ACADEMY OF ACHIEVEMENT
http://www.achievement.org

The goal of this tour is to instill in your students the inspiration, encouragement, and will to achieve by introducing them to the famous and not-so-famous men and women who have helped shape the twentieth century. Students have the option of choosing a successful person or a quality needed for success by walking through the appropriate gallery. For example, the *Gallery of Achievement* contains the halls of art, business, public service, science and exploration, sports, or the American dream. Each hall has audio, video, and written interviews with such notables as Johnny Cash, John Grisham, Henry Kravits, Willie Brown, Rosa Parks, Robert Ballard, Chuck Yeager, and Jules Irving. In the halls of passion, vision, preparation, courage, perseverance, and integrity, your students will hear some of the residents discuss their views on these qualities. For example, Robert Ballard will discuss the personality traits that allowed him to locate the Titanic. There is also a library where people discuss the books that made a difference in their lives, as well as a virtual book club where students can see which books are recommended by people such as Elie Wiesel. The library includes not only book reviews but also biographies, photographs, and audio interviews with authors such as R. L. Stine.

VAN DER ROHE, LUDWIG MIES
See Chapter 2—Bauhaus School of Architecture.

VAN GOGH, VINCENT
See Chapter 6—Art Museums—Vincent Van Gogh Information Gallery.

WALKER, C. J.
See Chapter 1—Women's History—National Register of Historic Places.

WASHINGTON, HAROLD
See Chapter 3—United States—Illinois—Chicago's Graveyards.

WELLES, ORSON
See Chapter 1—U.S. History—PBS American Experience Series.

WHARTON, EDITH
See Chapter 1—Women's History—National Register of Historic Places.

WILDER, LAURA INGALLS
See Chapter 7—Language Arts and Literature—Little House on the Prairie.

WILLIAMS, TENNESSEE
See Chapter 3—United States—Louisiana—New Orleans.

WRIGHT, FRANK LLOYD
See Chapter 2—Prairie School of Architecture.

YEAGER, CHARLES
See Chapter 1—Military History—United States Air Force.

Index

Abacus, 91
Abzug, Bella, 19
Adams, Abagail, 19
Advertising, 83–84
Agricultural Scavenger Hunt, 47
Akkadian Language, 3
Alaska, 36
Albatross Project, 61
Alcott, Louisa May, 117
Alexanderson, Ernst, 108
Allen, Red, 79
Alligators, 56
Alpacas, 48
Altgeld, John Peter, 38
Alvarez, Luis, 108
Amazonia, 29, 46
American Currency Exhibit, 14
American Landmarks, 35
American Museum of Natural History, 57
American Sheep Industry Association, 52
American West, 13–14
Amiens Cathedral, 24
Amish, 49
Amusement Park Industry, 14
Anatomy, 95
Ancient Civilizations, 1–2, 23, 72, 72, 80
Animals of the Arctic, 56
Animation, 67
Anne Hopkins Wien Elementary School, 36
Anthony, Susan B., 19
Antoinette, Marie, 4
Arboretums, 58–60
Archeology, 96
Archimedia Project, 23
Architecture, Alternative, 21–22
Architecture, American, 22–23
Architecture, Ancient, 23, 26
Architecture, Anglo-Norman, 24
Architecture, Art Noveau, 25
Architecture, Bauhaus School, 24
Architecture, Castles and Cathedrals, 24–25
Architecture, European, 26–27
Architecture, Gothic, 24, 26
Architecture, Old Rus, 25
Architecture, Prairie School, 28
Arctic, 56
Armstrong, Edwin, 108
Armstrong, Louis, 39
Armstrong, Neil, 9

Art Appreciation, 67
Art Lessons, 68
Art Museums, 69–71
Arthurian Legend, 75
Ask an Expert, 118
Ask Dr. Universe, 104
AT&T Labs, 89
Australia, 30
AutoCAD Modeling, 23
Automotive Industry, 85
Aviation, Aeronautics, & Aerospace, 9, 96–97

Ballard, Robert, 107, 139
Band Aids and Blackboards, 111
Barcelona, 27
Barkley Sound Expedition, 64
Barnyard Buddies, 48
Barton, Clara, 9
Basketball Hall of Fame, 112
Basie, Count, 79
Basque Region, 30
Bats, 56–57
Bauhaus School, 24
Bechet, Sidney, 39
Bell, Alexander, 107–108
Benny Goodsport, 112
Berg, Morris, 35
Bering, Vitus, 6
Berry, Chuck, 7–14
Berry, Martha, 15
Beverly Birks Couture Collection, 71
Big Bend National Park, 61
Bini, Dante, 21
Biology, 92–99
Biosphere 2, 100
Birds, 44, 61–62
Blackhawk Automotive Museum, 85
Blume, Judy, 119
Bly, Nellie, 17
Boone, Daniel, 14
Booth, John Wilkes, 132
Botanic Gardens, 58–60
Botany, 10–15
Bowie, James, 14
Brazil, 29, 30, 46
Breed, Clara, 6
Brett, Jan, 119
Bristlecone Pine, 55

British Columbia, 6
British Royal Navy, 6
Brooklyn Botanic Garden, 58
Bryant, Gridley, 23
Buffalo Soldiers, 19
Bullfinch, Charles, 22
Bureau of Land Management, 62
Burnham, Daniel, 38
Butterflies, 62–63

Cabrillo National Monument, 36
Calamity Jane, 13
Calculating Machines, 92
California, 36–37
California Energy Commission, 10–14
California State Automobile Association, 112
Camelot Project, 75
Canadian Animal Health Institute, 47
Canadian Broadcasting Corporation, 78, 104
Captain Zoom's Math Adventure, 92
Capote, Truman, 39
Carnegie, Andrew, 17
Carnegie Hall, 80
Carson, Christopher Houston (Kit), 14
Cartooning, 68
Cash, Johnny, 139
Cassidy, Butch, 13
Castles and Cathedrals, 24–25
Caves, 65
Central Intelligence Agency, 35
Cerf, Vinton, 108
Cermak, Anton, 38
Chateau of Versailles, 4, 26
Chemical Carousel, 97
Chemistry, 97, 98
Cherokee Tribe, 11, 15
Chicago Cultural Center, 26
Chicago Graveyards, 38
Chief Chickaumauga, 11
China, Republic of, 31
Civil Rights, 113
Civil Rights Movement, 40
Civil War, 8–9, 15, 38
Clark, William, 15
Cleburne, Patrick, 15
Coal Mining, 85–86
Cochran, Jaqueline, 10
Cody, William, 14, 122
Cold War, 17
Collins, Bootsy, 78
Colorado, 13
Columbian Exposition, 3

Columbus, Christopher, 1
Coney Island, 14
Conflict Resolution, 41, 113
Connecticut, 65
Cook, James, 6
Corn World, 48
County Fair, 48
Cousteau, Jacques, 122
Cray, Seymour, 107
CreatabiliToys, 83
Crime Prevention, 113, 114
Crockett, Davy, 14
Cuneiform Writing, 3
Currency, 8–10
Cytogenetics Gallery, 97

DNA Testing, 113
Dale, Dick, 78
Dart, Joseph, 17
Darwin, Charles, 32
De Gaulle, Charles, 4
Department of Justice, 113
Devereaux, Mrs. James, 9
Devonian Botanic Garden, 59
Disabilities, 57, 91, 111
Doctor Rabbits No Cavities Clubhouse, 113
Dogs, 57
Domino, Antoine (Fats), 39
Donavan, William, 35
Donkeys, Miniature, 51
Donner Party, 17
Drake, Sir Francis, 6
Drugs, Alcohol, and Tobacco, 113–115
Durham Cathedral and Castle, 24
Dust Bowl, 17

Earhart, Amelia, 124
Earp, Wyatt, 13
Earth and Environmental Education, 100–103
Earthquakes, 63, 102
Ecuador, 31
Edison, Thomas, 108, 125
Eggs, 50
Egypt, 31–32
Eiffel Tower, 26
Einstein, Albert, 125
Elmslie, George, 28
Endangered Species, 57–58
England, Medieval, 7
Environmental Protection Agency, 101
Erie Canal, 17

Europe, Eastern, 25
Experience Music Project, 78

Family Farm Project, 49
Farmer's Almanac, 49
Fashion and Design, 71–72
Federal Bureau of Investigation, 113
Federal Reserve Bank, 14, 86–87
Fellig, Arthur, 74
Fender, Leo, 79
Fermi, Enrico, 38
Field, Marshall, 38
Fisher, Carl, 17
Fitzergerald, F. Scott, 126
4-H Kids Informational Dirt Road, 47
Food and Drug Administration, 113
Ford, Robert, 13
Ford Theater, 132
Forensics, 103, 113
Forestry, 106
Forrest, Nathan Bedford, 15
Forrester, Jay, 107
Fort Ethan Allen, 18
Fort McArthur Museum, 36
1492, 1
Fowl, 49
France, 32
French History, 4, 69
Frank, Anne, 126–127
Franklin, Benjamin, 35
Freud, Sigmund, 127

Galapagos Islands, 32
Galileo, 127
Gargoyles, 26
Gates, Bill, 107
Gaudi, Antoni, 27
Gemology, 72–73
Genetic Engineering, 98
Genetic Testing, 98
Genetics, 97–99
Georgia, 15
Gillespie, Dizzy, 79
Giraffe Project, 128
Glacier National Park, 63
Globe Theater, 12
Goats, 50
Goddard, Robert, 9
Gold Rush, 17
Goldberg, Reuben Lucius (Rube), 129
Goldstein Museum of Design, 71

Grain Industry, 17
Grant, Ulysses, 129
Great Day in Harlem, 79
Great Kiva Tour, 41
Greece Central School District, 34
Greek Costumes, 72
Greek Jewelry, 72
Greenhow, Rose O'Neal, 9
Greenland, 46
Greek and Roman Stagecraft, 80
Grisham, John, 139
Gropius, Walter, 24
Groveland Farm, 52
Guide Dogs, 57
Guitars, 78, 79
Gwinnett, Button, 15

Hearst, William Randolph, 17
Hendrix, Jimi, 78, 79
Hewlett, William, 108
Hill, Virginia, 35
History, French, 4
Holabird and Root, 23
Holliday, Doc, 13
Holocaust, 5, 126–127
Hummingbirds, 62

Idaho, 15
Illinois, 38
Illinois Department of Agriculture, 50
Indian Health Service, 114
Indiana, 39
Innovation Network, 107
Institute of Physics, 109
International Center of Photography, 74
International Trade, 84
Inventions, 107–108, 129
Inventure Place, 108
Irving, Jules, 139
Israel, 33
Istanbul, 23
Italy, 27, 127

James Younger Gang, 13
Jamestown, 15
Japan, 33
Japanese American Museum, 6
Japanese Gardens, 59, 60
Jazz, 79

Jefferson, Thomas, 22
Jewelry, 72–73
Jobs, Steve, 107
Joe Nightingale School, 37
Jurrassic Reef Park, 63

Kahlo, Frieda, 69
Kassiane, 19
Kinetic Sculptures, 73
Kravits, Henry, 139

La Salle, Rene, 7
Lafayette, James Armistead, 35
Lafitte, Jean, 39
Language Arts, 75–78
Latrobe, Benjamin, 22
Lawrence Berkeley National Laboratory, 109
Lawrence, T. E., 132
Le Notre, Andre, 4
Lewis, C. S., 128
Lewis and Clark Expedition, 15–16
Lewis, Meriwether, 15–16
Life, Universe and the Electron, 109
Lincoln, Abraham, 17, 132
Lincoln, Mary Todd, 9
Lincoln Memorial, 43
Literature, 75–78
Livestock, 50
Lone Ranger, 133
Loocootee Elementary School, 39
Look, Learn and Do, 105
Loons, 44
Louis XIV, 4, 7
Louisiana Purchase, 39
Louisiana State Museum, 16, 27, 39, 69, 72
Luxton Museum of the Plains Indians, 11

McArthur, Douglas, 36
McKane, John, 14
McKinley, 17
Machiavelli, 128
Madagascar, 3–35
Magnetics, 109
Maine, 65
Manufacturing, 85–86
Marconi, 107
Maritime History, 6–7
Maritime Museum of British Columbia, 6
Marsalis Family, 39

Massachusetts, 19
Masterson, Bat, 13
Math Games, 92
Math Online Gallery, 92
Math Trading Cards, 93
Mathematicians, 93
Medical Ethics, 103
Medieval England, 7
Metcalfe, Robert, 108
Meterology, 101
Metropolitan Museum of Art, 70
Meyer, Anne, 107
Miami Museum of Science, 105
Michelangelo, 12, 128
Michigan Department of Agriculture, 48
Medici Family, 128
Middle Ages, 7
Military History, 8–11, 15, 36, 37, 39
Miller, John, 134
Mineral Management Service of Alaska, 86
Mining and Mineral Management, 85–86
Minds Eye Monster Project, 76
Minnesota Historical Museum, 6
Mississippi Moundbuilders, 3
Mississippi River, 3
Missouri Botanical Garden, 60
Mitchell, General William, 9
Mitchell, Maria, 19
Mobiles, 73
Molecular Modeling, 98
Money, Banking and Economics, 86–88
Montana, 15
Moonlit Road, 77
Moose, 36
Moran, Thomas, 135
Morton, Jelly Roll, 39
Motion Picture Industry, 78
Mubarak, Hosney and Suzanne, 31–32
Museum of French History, 4
Museum of New York, 16
Museum of Photographic Arts, 74
Museum of Science and Industry, 86, 105
Music, 78–79
Muybridge, Eadweard James, 73

Naismith, James, 112
Namibia, 46
Napoleon, 4
Nassy, Josef, 5
National Budget Simulation, 87
National Crime Prevention Council, 114
National Gallery of Canada, 70

National Geographic Society, 45
National Highway Traffic Safety Admin., 114
National Institute on Drug Abuse, 115
National Inventors Hall of Fame, 108
National Pork Producer's Council, 51
National Register of Historic Places, 18, 19
Native Americans, 11, 15, 41
New Orleans, 27, 39
New Hampshire, 40
New Jersey, 40
New Mexico, 41
New York, 14, 16, 17, 19, 41–42, 58, 64
Newspapers and Magazines, 88
Nike Missile Site, 37
Nineteenth Century Industry, 17
Nirvana, 78
Noh Theater, 80
Normans, 8
North Hagerstown High School, 40
Nutrition Café, 11–12

Oak View Elementary School, 43
Odyssey, 2
Ohio Hokshichankiya Farm Community, 51
Oliver, Joe King, 139
Oral Hygiene, 113
Oregon Museum of Science, 106
Owens, Jessie, 38

Packard, David, 108
Paleontology, 108
Palladio, Andrea, 27
Palmer, Potter, 38
Particle Adventure, 109
Patents, 108
PBS American Experience Series, 17
Pearl Jam, 78
Pencils, 84
Percy, Walker, 39
Perseus Project, 2
Peru, 29
Pez Museum, 84
Phenology, 64
Photography, 73–74
Physics, 103–106, 109–110
Pinkerton, Allan, 38
Pineo Ridge Moraine, 65
Plains Indians, 11
Plane Math, 93
Pocahontas, 15
Pocantico Hills School, 42

Poetry, 76
Polymers, 98
Pony Express, 14
Pork, 51
Price, 7–14
Primary Grade Sites, 31, 39, 41, 3–36, 48, 53, 57, 65, 76, 77, 91, 112, 113, 114
Princeton University, 40
Pullman, George, 38
Purcell, William, 28
Puzzling Playground, 93

Q Radio, 79
Quandaries and Queries, 94
Queen Mary, 37

Radio, 78, 79, 107
Railroads, 17, 105
Rainbows, 102
Rainforest, 31
Raitt, Bonnie, 7–14
Ranch Tour, 53
Regia Anglorum, 7
Renaissance, 12
Revolutionary War, 15
Rickenbacker, Eddie, 9
Robotics, 110
Rogers, Will, 137
Rolfe, John, 15
Roller Coasters, 103
Rolling Stones, 79
Roosevelt, Theodore, 17
Royal British Navy, 6

Saint Gaudens, Augustus, 137
Salem Witch Trials, 17–18
Salmon, 62
Schultz, Charles, 138
SciTech, 109
Science, General, 103–106
Science Museum of London, 109
Science Museum of Minnesota, 106
Seuss, Dr., 138
Seymour, David, 74
Shakespeare, 77
Sheep, 52
Sherman, William Tecumseh, 15
Ship Wrecks, 6–7
Simon Wiesenthal Center, 5
Sistine Chapel, 12

Sloan Automotive Museum, 85
Slocum, Joshua, 6
Smith, John, 15
Smokey the Bear, 65
Social Security Administration, 87
Sonoran Desert, 62
Southwestern Arboretum, 60
Sports, 111
Stine, R. L., 139
Stonehenge, 26
Stowe, Harriet Beecher, 9
Sullivan, Louis, 28, 38
Sunflower Elementary School, 44

Technology, 89
Texas, 7, 18, 61
Texas A & M Agropolis, 52
Texas Historical Commission, 7
Theaters, 80
Theodore Tugboat, 77
Thompson, J. J., 109
Thompson, William Hale, 38
Tibet, 3–35
Tigers, 58
Time Magazine for Kids, 88
Tower of London, 12
Tower Lyrics Archive, 81
Travel Buddies, 34
Triple Nickels, 10
Tubman, Harriet, 42
20th Century Academy of Achievement, 139
20th Century Physics, 10–40
Twin Groves Junior High, 12

Ukraine, 25
Underground Railroad, 18, 42
United Nations, 42, 45
United States, 35–46
United States Air Force, 9
United States Fish and Wildlife Service, 58
United States History, 12–19, 39, 43, 132
United States Holocaust Museum, 5

United States Marshalls, 113
United States Treasury, 88

Van der Rohe, Ludwig Mies, 24
Van Gogh, Vincent, 70
Vermont, 18
Vietnam War, 17
Vikings, 7–8
Virginia, 15, 43
Virtual Fly, 99
Virtual Keeping House, 11–12

Walker, C. J., 19
War of 1812, 39
Warner Brothers Studios, 67
Washington, 15
Washington, Harold, 38
Washington D.C., 43
Water, Drinking, 10–15
Weekly Reader, 88
Wells, Orson, 17
Wharton, Edith, 19
Wheat Mania, 53
Wiesel, Elie, 139
Wilder, Laura Ingalls, 76
Wildflowers, 62
Williams, Tennessee, 39
Wisconsin, 44
Wisconsin Department of Natural Resource, 103
Women in the Arts, 71
Women's Airforce Service Pilots, 10
Women's History, 19
World War I, 10
World War II, 6, 10–11, 17
World Wide Words, 77
Wright Brothers, 17
Wright, Frank Lloyd, 28
Wyoming, 44

Yeager, Charles, 9, 139
Young, Lester, 79